MI DAILY DEVOTION

MI DAILY DEVOTION

100 Days of Love, Inspirations,
Encouragement, Encounter with God,
Self- Evaluation, Quiet time with God,
Challenges and Comfort

ELY ROQUE SAGANSAY

WestBow
PRESS
A DIVISION OF THOMAS NELSON

WestBow Press books may be ordered through booksellers or by contacting:

WestBow Press
A Division of Thomas Nelson
1663 Liberty Drive
Bloomington, IN 47403
www.westbowpress.com
1-(866) 928-1240

ISBN: 978-1-4497-1313-3 (sc)
ISBN: 978-1-4497-1347-8 (e)

Library of Congress Control Number: 2011923138

Edited by: Eliezer Dumala Sagansay, Ely Dumala
Sagansay JR, Eliel Lyn Dumala Sagansay
Photo: Ely R. Sagansay
Cover Designed: Eliel Lyn D. Sagansay

Printed in the United States of America
WestBow Press rev. date: 7/25/2011

DEDICATION

This devotional book is dedicated to the One who saved me and washed me with His precious Blood, my LORD and Savior Jesus Christ. To my loving wife Bermilin Dumala Sagansay, to my children: Eliezer, Ely Jr. Eliel Lyn and Elmer John (EJ). And to my church, the Philippine International Christian Church- Trenton, Michigan, thank you so much for your prayers and support. "TO GOD BE THE GLORY!"

was history." But on my part, it would be, "… and is HIS (The Lord's) STORY".

a abbreviation of MICHIGAN, but for me, it would n MY INSPIRATION. My Inspiration is God, His y family and you who reads and made some positive ts on Facebook in MI DAILY DEVOTION. It is re to be an inspiration to you and to be a channel 's blessings. God bless!!! ENJOY and share HIS

the res
the res

MI is a
also me
Word,
comme
my des
of Goc
STOR

FOREWO

MI DAILY DEVOTION was bo
Lord, not during my hay days, b
during my good days, but difficu
of the hospital for 9 months and
December 03, 2009 when I lost m
with my physical sickness and ;
emotional and spiritual struggles d
my life. We were also struggling fi
because my wife's employers mad
her job. The fear of being idle was
of losing my extra income adds up
so sick and at the same time, I lc
insurance from my job which re
situation physically, financially
those times, I received encouragi
great comments on Facebook f
comfort and encouraged me. I pr
who prayed for me and support i
I was also thinking of turning tl
in mind, I started posting positi
to be a blessing and an encoura;
like what people would say at the

SUNDAY- MI DAILY DEVOTION
(II Corinthians 5:21) (KJV)

AN EASTER MESSAGE...

21- "For He hath made Him to be sin for us, who knew no sin; that we might be made the righteousness of God in Him." (KJV)

THE PROCLAMATION OF THE LORD'S COMMAND... *(Leviticus 17:1-4)* 1- *"And the LORD* spake unto Moses, saying, 2- Speak unto Aaron, and unto his sons, and unto all the children of Israel, and say unto them; This is the thing which the LORD hath commanded, saying, 3- What man soever there be of the house of Israel, that killeth an ox, or lamb, or goat, in the camp, or that killeth it out of the camp, 4- And bringeth it not unto the door of the tabernacle of the congregation, to offer an offering unto the LORD before the tabernacle of the LORD; blood shall be imputed unto that man; he hath shed blood; and that man shall be cut off from among his people:"

THE PURPOSE OF THE LORD'S COMMAND... (Leviticus 17:5-6) 5- "To the end that the children of Israel may bring their sacrifices, which they offer in the open field, even that they may bring them unto the LORD, unto the door of the tabernacle of the congregation, unto the priest, and offer them for peace offerings unto the LORD. 6- And the priest shall sprinkle the blood upon the altar of the LORD at the door of the tabernacle of the congregation, and burn the fat for a sweet savour unto the LORD."

THE PUNISHMENT FOR DISOBEYING THE LORD'S COMMAND... (Leviticus 17:7-9) 7- "And they shall no more offer their sacrifices unto devils, after whom they have gone a whoring. This shall be a statute for ever unto them throughout their generations. 8- And thou shalt say unto them, Whatsoever man there be of the house of Israel, or of the strangers which sojourn among you, that offereth a burnt offering or sacrifice, 9- And bringeth it not unto the door of the tabernacle of the congregation, to offer it unto the LORD; even that man shall be cut off from among his people."

THE POWER OF THE BLOOD... It has power to *raise* us up from the grave. The shed Blood of the Lord Jesus Christ has power to *redeem* us from the law and sin. It has the power to make us *righteous* before God. I hope and pray that this daily reading will be a blessing to you as it is to me as I ponder on the Word of God. In (Hebrews 10: 4- 13) 4- "For it is not possible that the blood of bulls and of goats should take away sins. 5- Wherefore when he cometh into the world, he saith, Sacrifice and offering thou wouldest not, but a body hast thou prepared me: 6- In burnt offerings and sacrifices for sin thou hast had no pleasure. 7- Then said I, Lo, I come (in the volume of the book it is written of me,) to do thy will, O God. 8- Above when he said, Sacrifice and offering and burnt offerings and offering for sin thou wouldest not, neither hadst pleasure therein; which are offered by the law; 9- Then said he, Lo, I come to do thy will, O God. He taketh away the first, that he may establish the second. 10- By the which will we are sanctified through the offering of the body of Jesus Christ once for all. 11- And every priest standeth daily ministering and offering oftentimes the same sacrifices, which can never take away sins: 12- But this man, after he had offered one sacrifice for sins for ever, sat down on the right hand of God; 13- From henceforth expecting till his enemies be made his footstool."

MONDAY- MI DAILY DEVOTION
(Matthew 11: 28-30)

"COME... TAKE... LEARN..."

28- "Come unto me, all ye that labour and are heavy laden, and I will give you rest. 29- Take my yoke upon you, and learn of me; for I am meek and lowly in heart: and ye shall find rest unto your souls. 30- For my yoke is easy, and my burden is light."

When you have *no one to hold on to and help is not available*. When life gets complicated and everything does not go the way it should. When your heart breaks and it's just so much for you to take... Then your pain is unbearable and the problem is insurmountable, Jesus said: "Come unto me, all ye that labour and are heavy laden, and I will give you rest."

When *no one wants to take you and everybody tries to break you*. When your brain is drained and you're stressed out 'cause life is a messed. And you're tired and dried and you have no one to guide you. You wanted to go up, but the road is too narrow for you, Jesus said: "Take my yoke upon you, and learn of me; for I am meek and lowly in heart: and ye shall find rest unto your souls."

When life is hard and your freedom is barred. If the road is rough and everything is tough. Your soul longed for comfort and comfort is gone. You desperately longed for peace in your heart as happiness and joy anon. When everything is dark and the fort is black. Your lighthouse is broken and your soul is darkened... Jesus said: "For my yoke is easy, and my burden is light." ElyRS

You will never understand all these until you've been there or you are there already. God is able, but are you available? Are you available to come unto the throne of grace? God is able, but do you have faith like mustard seed? Are you like the hopeless and helpless blind men who followed the Lord Jesus Christ, the Son of David? (Matthew 9: 27-30) "And when Jesus departed thence, two blind men followed him, crying, and saying, Thou son of David, have mercy on us. 28- And when he was come into the house, the blind men came to him: and Jesus saith unto them, Believe ye that I am able to do this? They said unto him, Yea, Lord. 29- Then touched he their eyes, saying, According to your faith be it unto you. 30- And their eyes were opened; and Jesus straitly charged them, saying, See that no man know it." God wanted for us to *come* to Him in prayer. He also wanted to for us to *take* His Word by faith in our hearts, to *learn* His ways and *learn* from our trials and sufferings.

Notice what Peter said in (I Peter 5:6-7) "Humble yourselves therefore under the mighty hand of God, that he may exalt you in due time: 7- Casting all your care upon him; for he careth for you."

TUESDAY- MI DAILY DEVOTION
(Genesis 13: 8)

LOT..., DO YOU HAVE A PROBLEM WITH ME?

That could be the question of Abraham to Lot.

8- "And Abram said unto Lot, Let there be no strife, I pray thee, between me and thee, and between my herdmen and thy herdmen; for we be brethren."

The conflict between Abraham and Lot was so bad to the point that they have to separate their ways. While the same blood and DNA flows though their nerves and bodies; it was very obvious that the spirit that flows through their lives were so different. It's so ironic that they were God's children, next door neighbors and they were related, but they submitted themselves to such conflict, where they have to separate ways. I was just thinking about this and sometimes it made me believe that there's no such thing as leadership conflict in any church, groups or organizations. Conflicts could be caused by pride, arrogance, jealousy and envy. And let me say this in general- *SIN*. I believe that Satan has a big part to any conflicts in churches, at homes or Christian organizations. Poverty, prosperity and power struggles are sometimes some of the common causes of conflicts not just in the Christian community, but also in some homes and countries as well. (Genesis 13:6-8) "6- And the land was not able to bear them, that they might dwell together: for their substance was great, so that they could not dwell together. 7- And there was a strife between the herdmen of Abram's cattle and the herdmen of Lot's cattle: and the Canaanite and the Perizzite dwelled then in the land. 8- And Abram said unto Lot, Let there be no strife, I pray thee, between me and thee, and between my herdmen and thy herdmen; for we be brethren."

Abraham and Lot's problems were minor, but Abraham was so smart that he did not let their little issues go unresolved before he took a step to iron them out. When I took a seminar to be a security officer here in Michigan, one of the things that I've learned was about prevention. Fire prevention and prevention against robbery, murders, accidents and other tragedies and man- made calamities. Abraham did exactly what was right and fair. Actually, Abraham made the right decision and he made the right and good judgment by letting Lot go with his blessings. He resolved the issues before it went from bad to worst. I hope and pray that we will do the same. Some people may have asked this question, did Abraham let go of the problem, let go of sin or let go of Lot?

(Genesis 13:9) - "Is not the whole land before thee? Separate thyself, I pray thee, from me: if thou wilt take the left hand, then I will go to the right; or if thou depart to the right hand, then I will go to the left."

WEDNESDAY- MI DAILY DEVOTION
(Genesis 13: 6)

LOT AND ABRAHAM- DID YOU HAVE CONFLICTS BECAUSE OF PETS, PEOPLE, PROPERTIES OR POWER?

That could be the question for Abraham and Lot.

6- "And the land was not able to bear them, that they might dwell together: for their substance was great, so that they could not dwell together."

Abraham and Lot both know what it means to be poor and needy and to live in poverty." (Genesis 12:9-10)

We can be in a low profile in spite of power, prosperity and wealth, if we know what it means to be poor and needy and if we have experienced poverty in our lifetime. There are those who are humbled by the Lord through the success that God has given them and the blessings of prosperity. Abraham had an SS issue, which means *Strife* and *Separation*. So, what could be the reasons of their strife and separation?

Insecurity could be one of the factors of their strife and their servants' strife. Let me call it (the Insecurity) issue. "The Prevalent Sin" in churches, among pastors and organizations and even businesses. I don't know how it would look like if Christians would work together in the same cause and with the same spirit. (Psalms 133:1-3) 1- "Behold, how good and how pleasant it is for brethren to dwell together in unity! 2- It is like the precious ointment upon the head, that ran down upon the beard, even Aaron's beard: that went down to the skirts of his garments; 3- As the dew of Hermon, and

You will have burdens in accumulating them and the fear of losing them and the fear of keeping them as well as the temptation in over using them. You will also have the danger of abusing by over using your wealth. Abraham's wealth was in God, from God and it's of God for sure. That was indeed God's blessing because He added no burdens to it. (Proverbs 10:22) "The blessing of the LORD, it maketh rich, and he addeth no sorrow with it." God said to Abram, "*I will bless thee…*"

It's good to be rich and prosperous, but don't trade your love ones for the sake of money or for your love of money. Your love ones are God's gift to you and money could be the world's gift to you. It breaks my heart when I think of those who sacrificed or have left their loved ones for money. And I don't understand it when parents will have all their time for business, for making money and they don't have time for their family. And on the other side of the road, you have families who fight, were separated and disconnected because of power and wealth. Apostle Paul has a good advice for all of us. (I Timothy 6:9-10) 9-"But they that will be rich fall into temptation and a snare, and into many foolish and hurtful lusts, which drown men in destruction and perdition. 10- For the love of money is the root of all evil: which while some coveted after, they have erred from the faith, and pierced themselves through with many sorrows."

FRIDAY- MI DAILY DEVOTION
(Genesis 13:1-12)

LOT AND ABRAHAM- "WERE YOU LOSING OR MISSING YOUR T-I-M-E-R?"

7- "And there was a strife between the herdmen of Abram's cattle and the herdmen of Lot's cattle: and the Canaanite and the Perizzite dwelled then in the land. 8- And Abram said unto Lot, Let there be no strife, I pray thee, between me and thee, and between my herdmen and thy herdmen; for we be brethren. 9- Is not the whole land before thee? separate thyself, I pray thee, from me: if thou wilt take the left hand, then I will go to the right; or if thou depart to the right hand, then I will go to the left."

That could be a good question for Abraham and Lot. But what do I mean of the word "timer"? Do they have some kind of a watch or clock back then already? It's actually an acronym and we will talk about the acronym T-I-M-E-R which is very relevant to many Christians and churches. Some of the Christians I know including pastors and missionaries have lost their T-I-M-E-R already and it's so sad.

The problem of Abraham and Lot could be the following things that many of Abrahams and Lots of this generation have lost as well.

T-I-M-E-R

T-testimony- You have lost your testimony because of money, immorality or you did not stand for what is right, moral or

11

holy. You also compromised your faith, the Word of God for some reason or reasons.

I-inspiration- Instead of an inspiration to their herdsmen and servants, they became a stumbling blocks. People are watching you making bad decisions instead of being an inspiration.

M-momentum- They lost their momentum because they were busy with their wealth, solving their herdsmen issues and at the same time they were busy solving their grief and separation.

E-evangelism- It was so difficult for them to share the Word of God while their people were watching them with their confrontation regarding their issues on wealth and people.

R-respect- Don't lost that important thing in life-"respect". If you lost your respect from your family circle or subordinate or church members, a good friend of mine said; "you're done, man"! We need to win and gain their respect by being a man or woman God wanted us to be. Learn from Apostle Paul in his letter to young Timothy. (I Timothy 2:10-12) 10- "Ye are witnesses, and God also, how holily and justly and unblameably we behaved ourselves among you that believe: 11- As ye know how we exhorted and comforted and charged every one of you, as a father doth his children, 12- That ye would walk worthy of God, who hath called you unto his kingdom and glory."

SATURDAY- MI DAILY DEVOTION
(Genesis 13:9- 11)

LOT... YOU HAVE LIVED UP TO THAT NAME!

9- "Is not the whole land before thee? separate thyself, I pray thee, from me: if thou wilt take the left hand, then I will go to the right; or if thou depart to the right hand, then I will go to the left. 10- And Lot lifted up his eyes, and beheld all the plain of Jordan, that it was well watered everywhere, before the LORD destroyed Sodom and Gomorrah, even as the garden of the LORD, like the land of Egypt, as thou comest unto Zoar. 11- Then Lot chose him all the plain of Jordan; and Lot journeyed east: and they separated themselves the one from the other."

LOT

L- *LIBERAL*- Meaning of Liberal- "not strict or rigorous; free; not literal: *a liberal interpretation of a rule.* According to Dictionary.com

Lot was so liberal in his stand on moral issues, in his dealings with his family, in his Biblical stands and his lifestyle as well. He was a leftists or on the negative side of the wings. No wonder Lot messed up his family's life and he lost the respect of his children and his wife. (Genesis 19:5; 8-9) 5- "And they called unto Lot, and said unto him, Where are the men which came in to thee this night? bring them out unto us, that we may know them."

8- "Behold now, I have two daughters which have not known man; let me, I pray you, bring them out unto you, and do ye to them as is good in your eyes: only unto these men do nothing; for therefore came they under the shadow of my roof. 9- And they said, Stand back. And they said again, This one fellow came in to sojourn, and he will needs be a judge: now will we deal worse with thee, than with them. And they pressed sore upon the man, even Lot, and came near to break the door."

O- *OPPORTUNISTS*- My own interpretation of opportunists: taking advantage of something from someone for personal gain and interests. The opportunists are the ones who are taking advantage of the opportunity, up to the point of using other people's rights and possessions for selfish motivation and selfish desires. And it's very obvious in Lot's life. You can be an opportunist in a positive way and Godly way. You can also be an opportunist for God's glory. (Genesis 13:1-6; 10-12)

T- *TREASURE/S CENTERED*- Lot's life was centered on treasures. He went with Abraham with riches in mind. He separated himself from Abraham with the good property and worldly riches in mind. And his life was centered on wealth. You can know a person's priorities even in his decisions. Your perspective in life will help determine your future. Man's perspective in life will show in his daily decision making process. Are you God-Centered, Gold Centered or Gain Centered? (Matthew 6:33) "But seek ye first the kingdom of God, and his righteousness; and all these things shall be added unto you."

SUNDAY- MI DAILY DEVOTION
(Titus 1:1)

PAUL- PROUD TO BE AN APOSTLE OF THE LORD JESUS CHRIST

1- "Paul, a servant of God, and an apostle of Jesus Christ, according to the faith of God's elect, and the acknowledging of the truth which is after godliness;"

"Paul an apostle of Jesus Christ...," This was Paul's introductions in his writings to some of his Epistle. (Colossians 1:1; Ephesians 1:1) It seems that Paul was proud (but not boastful) of his title as an Apostle of the Lord Jesus Christ and I'm very much sure that his credentials were unquestionable. Paul has the BIG 5 "C's" as servant of God. Paul was: *CONVERTED, COMMITTED, CALLED, COMMISSIONED and COMMANDED.* It was the Lord Jesus Christ Himself who ordained him a preacher of the gospel while Paul was on his way to Damascus (Acts 9:1-9). Paul was a preacher of Christ who desired not to build his own kingdom, but the kingdom of God. It's opposite to what we're seeing now as you observed the lifestyle and the kind of life many "so called" preachers of the gospel of the Lord Jesus Christ. You see some tele-evangelists and preachers who lives not as servants of God, but servants of man, manna or methods. (Titus 1:1) "Paul, a servant of God, and an apostle of Jesus Christ, according to the faith of God's elect, and the acknowledging of the truth which is after godliness;" I like the attitude of Apostle Paul. In (I Timothy 1:2) "Unto Timothy, my own son in the faith: Grace, mercy, and peace, from God our Father and Jesus Christ our Lord." He calls Timothy his own son, because

Paul was instrumental on Timothy's conversion. And Paul trained Timothy and prepared him for the ministry like a father putting his son into a strict discipline to prepare him for service. He was a son who served with him in the gospel of the Lord Jesus Christ. Now Paul here was talking about his other son-Titus. (Titus 1:4) "To Titus, mine own son after the common faith: Grace, mercy, and peace, from God the Father and the Lord Jesus Christ our Saviour." Do you know that every Christians or believers of the Lord Jesus Christ, we also have the "BIG 5 C's" from the time we were born in the family of God? We know we were born again, but we're not aware of our calling. As Christians, we were called to serve and to preach. We were commanded by the Lord to "GO". God expect us to be committed to His cause. Salvation is free for all, but it costs the Father His one and only Son- the Lord Jesus Christ. And it costs Christ His life, suffering and pain beyond our imaginations. Christian's hope is in the Lord. We have our hope in the foundation which God has built even before God created the world. The Lord called us and He wants for us to continue in His grace and service and be proud of our calling. The common saying in Christian circle is- "Keep on keeping on…" Notice the testimony of Apostle Paul in (II Timothy 2:10-12) "But thou hast fully known my doctrine, manner of life, purpose, faith, longsuffering, charity, patience,11- Persecutions, afflictions, which came unto me at Antioch, at Iconium, at Lystra; what persecutions I endured: but out of them all the Lord delivered me. 12- Yea, and all that will live godly in Christ Jesus shall suffer persecution."

MONDAY- MI DAILY DEVOTION
(II Timothy 1:9)

THE SOLID FOUNDATION, THE SOLID ROCK-
JESUS!!!

9- "Who hath saved us, and called us with an holy calling, not according to our works, but according to his own purpose and grace, which was given us in Christ Jesus before the world began,"

The hope of eternal life… The grace, mercy, love and the peace of the Lord Jesus Christ were the components or the reasons that made the gift of eternal life so easy to believe in. We have a promised to discover and we can be certain of what we have in Christ Jesus our Lord. This is God's general blessing for the lost world. We can have God's salvation through the death, burial and resurrection of the Lord Jesus Christ. But someone has to decide to believe in and to receive that promised by faith in the Lord Jesus Christ. You can't have that life unless you take a step of faith. Notice here the hope of our salvation is the Solid Rock. This hymn has ministered to my heart:

"My hope is built on nothing less
Than Jesus' blood and righteousness.
I dare not trust the sweetest frame
but wholly trust in Jesus' Name.

On Christ the solid Rock I stand
all other ground is sinking sand
all other ground is sinking sand.

His oath, His covenant, His blood
Support me in the whelming flood.
When all around my soul gives way
He then is all my Hope and Stay." By: Edward Mote

Praise God!!! Our salvation is in the good, right and Solid Foundation which is the Lord Jesus Christ, our blessed Hope. He is the Rock of Ages. Why would you trust and even entrust your life to a man made religion, when you have a Heaven made religion through our Lord Jesus Christ. Why would you put your trust and even entrust your life and the life to come to something, when you can put your trust to Someone- Jesus our Savior. Why would you love the sinking sand, when you have the Solid Rock and He is the King of Glory, the Lord God Almighty! (Isaiah 28:16) "Therefore thus saith the Lord GOD, Behold, I lay in Zion for a foundation a stone, a tried stone, a precious corner stone, a sure foundation: he that believeth shall not make haste." (I Corinthians 3:10-11) "According to the grace of God which is given unto me, as a wise masterbuilder, I have laid the foundation, and another buildeth thereon. But let every man take heed how he buildeth thereupon. 11- For other foundation can no man lay than that is laid, which is Jesus Christ."

TUESDAY- MI DAILY DEVOTION
(Psalm 33:18, 22; 71:5, 14)

"FOR IN GOD DO I HOPE"

"18-Behold, the eye of the LORD is upon them that fear him, upon them that hope in his mercy; 22- Let thy mercy, O LORD, be upon us, according as we hope in thee." 5- "For thou art my hope, O Lord GOD: thou art my trust from my youth. 14- But I will hope continually, and will yet praise thee more and more."

We can hope in God while we're serving Him. We serve Him as King of kings. As God's children, we were called to serve and even in our service to the King, we have hope in Him alone. (Ephesians 1:18-19) We serve Him with great expectation. Even in the least and greatest service you have for our God, we can always place that expectation in His hands. We can always expect God to work in us and through us. And expect something great from God in your service to Him. (Ephesians 4:4) "There is one body, and one Spirit, even as ye are called in one hope of your calling;" We are serving God who is the God of hope. And He is the God who gave us hope, so we can encourage those who are hopeless. (Romans 15:13-14) "Now the God of hope fill you with all joy and peace in believing, that ye may abound in hope, through the power of the Holy Ghost. 14- And I myself also am persuaded of you, my brethren, that ye also are full of goodness, filled with all knowledge, able also to admonish one another." As we serve Him in this hopeless generation, let's look up to God with great expectation and exhortation for our brothers and sisters in the Lord, so we could encourage others also. We hope in God, so we can be an example to others. We magnify God in our lives and set an example for others to follow. Our *expectation, exhortation and example* should shade hope to the hopeless and should help and encourage others, both believers and non-believers as well. Let everybody know that there is hope and that hope is just a prayer away from where you are. We are living in a generation where people wanted everything instant, including "hope". But God wants to teach us patient. (Ecclesiastes 9:3-4) "This is an evil among all things that are done under the sun, that there is one event unto all: yea, also the heart of the sons of men is full of evil, and madness is in their heart while they live, and after that they go to the dead. 4- For to him that is joined to all the living there is hope: for a living dog is better than a dead lion." We can also hope in God for our daily sustenance. (Lamentations 3:24, 26) "The LORD is my portion, saith my soul; therefore will I hope in him. 26- It is good that a man should both hope and quietly wait for the salvation of the LORD." We can hope and pray for our daily needs and God is pleased if we trust Him for our cares and burdens. We can place everything in His hands and His provision. We can put our trust in God's love, mercy and grace. God can do it, if you only believe in Him. (Psalms 147:10-11) "He delighteth not in the strength of the horse: he taketh not pleasure in the legs of a man. 11- The LORD taketh pleasure in them that fear him, in those that hope in his mercy."

WEDNESDAY- MI DAILY DEVOTION
(Deuteronomy 1:20-21)

"DON'T BE LIKE 'EM!!!"

20- "And I said unto you, Ye are come unto the mountain of the Amorites, which the LORD our God doth give unto us. 21- Behold, the LORD thy God hath set the land before thee: go up and possess it, as the LORD God of thy fathers hath said unto thee; fear not, neither be discouraged."

There are several causes and reasons that drive people in different moods, in having negative and positive mind set and having negative or positive attitudes as well. There are dangers in our Christian life. And anything that we stored in into our heart or sub-conscious can spark in a second and could cause us to react negatively based on what we have stored in into our hearts and minds. Sometimes it's so easy for us to get stressed out due to what's going on in our heart and mind. Christian life and life itself is a roller coaster. One of the things that caused us to go down to the lowest level in our roller coaster ride in life is "discouragement". "Discourage" means "dishearten" "to dissuade" "dismayed". The Bible said, "Fear not, be not afraid nor be dismayed…" I just want to remind you that we have the same assurance and promise from the Lord whether in good times or bad times. (Joshua 1:9) "Have not I commanded thee? Be strong and of a good courage; be not afraid, neither be thou dismayed: for the LORD thy God is with thee whithersoever thou goest." Being a pastor for quite a while, every time I look at the ministry in the flesh or human perspective, the instinct or natural reactions is to get discourage instead of more trust and love for God. And we have the same reactions and instinct when we look at the family problems and financial problems that we have especially in these difficult times. But we should remember that the Lord will not give us trials, sufferings and problems to discourage us or to destroy us or cause us to get depress, but to help us see life in the eye of faith and love. During the time of Moses, they have the same problems- they have people that are so negative. I know of Christians and even leaders who are so negative. I am into praying, thinking and planning, but I'm not the kind of person who wants a very clear revelation from heaven before I make a decision or jump into a project. I like to take risks and do something different. But I make sure that I take the responsibility if it fails and give God the glory if it succeeds. I don't consider failure a total failure. I look at failures as lessons to learn and good experiences. I have observed this from different people; I noticed this that the kids who grew up in a very negative environment or parents… they tend to be negative, afraid to take a risk, insecure and they easily get discouraged. This happened during the time of Moses and it's still happening today. Don't be like 'em!!!

In (Numbers 32:6-9) "And Moses said unto the children of Gad and to the children of Reuben, Shall your brethren go to war, and shall ye sit here? 7- And wherefore discourage ye the heart of the children of Israel from going over into the land which the LORD hath given them? 8- Thus did your fathers, when I sent them from Kadeshbarnea to see the land. 9- For when they went up unto the valley of Eshcol, and saw the land, they discouraged the heart of the children of Israel, that they should not go into the land which the LORD had given them."

THURSDAY- MI DAILY DEVOTION
(I Samuel 30:3- 6)

"BUT DAVID ENCOURAGED HIMSELF IN THE LORD"

3- "So David and his men came to the city, and, behold, it was burned with fire; and their wives, and their sons, and their daughters, were taken captives. 4- Then David and the people that were with him lifted up their voice and wept, until they had no more power to weep. 5- And David's two wives were taken captives, Ahinoam the Jezreelitess, and Abigail the wife of Nabal the Carmelite. 6- And David was greatly distressed; for the people spake of stoning him, because the soul of all the people was grieved, every man for his sons and for his daughters: but David encouraged himself in the LORD his God."

Family problems and conflicts always lead to discouragement and disappointment. It is natural to get discourage and disappointed, but to dwell in them should not be the case. The seventh leading cause of death among men is suicide and sixteenth on women. And violence, physical and sexual abused is one of the factors of suicide in the family as according to National Institute of Mental Health in their web site at www.nimh.nih.gov. Family problems and conflicts is one of the reasons why so many teenagers who get discouraged turned to sex and drugs as substitute or comfort and reliever.

David's problems caused him to get discouraged and it was his own doing and bad decisions. He was supposed to just stay at home. I believe David was trying to put everything on his shoulder when he left and joined the troops, not knowing that the Amalekites invaded the whole city and captured his people including his own family. (I Samuel 30:5) "And David's two wives were taken captives, Ahinoam the Jezreelitess, and Abigail the wife of Nabal the Carmelite." There are those who live in poverty and they get used to it already. I was telling a friend one day that those who lived in poverty, they either don't know that they're so poor or they don't know what it means to be rich. They know what it means to be rich, but they just don't know how to get there. Some poor people put the blame on luck, fate, politics and others they put the blame on themselves. There are those who are poor and needy and they're discouraged because of their financial situation and difficulties. And there are those who get discouraged just by watching the poor and needy and watching those who are going through financial difficulties. Watching people on the other side of the world starved to death is very discouraging. But, whether you're rich or poor, you have millions of dollars or you're a bum, we all have problems and we will soon get discouraged. One good thing with David is that, he knows how to encourage himself. If we were in his shoes, we will definitely get discourage too. But imagine yourself like David trying to tap your back and talking to yourself (Soliloquy-an utterance or discourse by a person who is talking to himself or herself. Dictionary. com) to encourage yourself and saying; "It's alright, because everything will be alright. God will be there for you to help and sustain you." (I Samuel 30:6) "And David was greatly distressed; for the people spake of stoning him, because the soul of all the people was grieved, every man for his sons and for his daughters: but David encouraged himself in the LORD his God."

FRIDAY- MI DAILY DEVOTION
(I Samuel 30:4)

"DAVID HAD NO MORE POWER TO WEEP"

4- "Then David and the people that were with him lifted up their voice and wept, until they had no more power to weep."

Have you ever been so discourage and the reason for your discouragement was because of your friends or love ones. (Deuteronomy 1:26-30) "Notwithstanding ye would not go up, but rebelled against the commandment of the LORD your God:" Rebellion against God's people could cause us to get discourage and cause those around us to get discourage too. The same old, old story, the Israelites rebelled against God and the people were affected. And the next thing you'll hear- people will murmur and they'll start to think, say and do negative things. Sometimes like the Israelites of old, they began to be judge-mental. I wonder how many of us have experienced such... verses 27-28 "And ye murmured in your tents, and said, Because the LORD hated us, he hath brought us forth out of the land of Egypt, to deliver us into the hand of the Amorites, to destroy us. 28- Whither shall we go up? our brethren have discouraged our heart, saying, The people is greater and taller than we; the cities are great and walled up to heaven; and moreover we have seen the sons of the Anakims there."

We praise God for people who have this kind of attitude, always positive, submissive and an encourager: verses 29-30 "Then I said unto you, Dread not, neither be afraid of them. 30- The LORD your God which goeth before you, he shall fight for you, according to all that he did for you in Egypt before your eyes;" Be careful with friends and brethren who make you discourage due to negative remarks, advice or counsel and unbiblical advices. If you are going to use your imagination, picture in your mind (I Samuel 30:4) "Then David and the people that were with him lifted up their voice and wept, until they had no more power to weep." You were shouting, weeping and keep on yelling until you lost your voice and you have lost your strength and power even just to weep. Remember that last failure, bad experiences, trials, suffering etc… and you wept until there was nothing to weep. You cried out to God until you were dried, hopeless and empty and you can't even pray anymore. Remember that last failure you have at school or work? Have you ever looked back to that ambitions and goals that never happened? And you were so discouraged and just so dried and exhausted. You are not alone, David went through those and millions of people are going through the same situations at this very moment. But notice what David went through in (Psalm 69:2-3; 20) "I sink in deep mire, where there is no standing: I am come into deep waters, where the floods overflow me. 3- I am weary of my crying: my throat is dried: mine eyes fail while I wait for my God. 20- Reproach hath broken my heart; and I am full of heaviness: and I looked for some to take pity, but there was none; and for comforters, but I found none." In (II Samuel 22:2-3) "And he said, The LORD is my rock, and my fortress, and my deliverer; 3- The God of my rock; in him will I trust: he is my shield, and the horn of my salvation, my high tower, and my refuge, my saviour; thou savest me from violence."

SATURDAY- MI DAILY DEVOTION
(I Samuel 30: 6)

"HOW DO YOU REACT TO YOUR DISCOURAGEMENT?"

6- "And David was greatly distressed; for the people spake of stoning him, because the soul of all the people was grieved, every man for his sons and for his daughters: but David encouraged himself in the LORD his God."

Some people began to have a wrong attitude toward God when they're discouraged. I believe David did the right thing when he just wept and shout and cried really hard before he took a moved or made the decisions for his people and his family. Don't make any minor or major decisions when you're discouraged. What should be the attitude of Christians toward discouragement? Here are some few tips, reminders and encouragement for you:

Don't be afraid, but be courageous. (Joshua 1:8-9) "This book of the law shall not depart out of thy mouth; but thou shalt meditate therein day and night, that thou mayest observe to do according to all that is written therein: for then thou shalt make thy way prosperous, and then thou shalt have good success. 9- Have not I commanded thee? Be strong and of a good courage; be not afraid, neither be thou dismayed: for the LORD thy God is with thee whithersoever thou goest."

Remember that God shall go before you and shall fight for you. (Deuteronomy 1:29-30)

God will carry us and He will carry us through. The Bible said, "The Lord thy God bare thee..." I remember the very popular song by a good friend of mine, Mr. Scott Wesley Brown: *"HE WILL CARRY YOU"*

> "There is no problem so big, God cannot solve it
> There is no mountain so tall, He cannot move it
> There is no storm so dark, God cannot calm it
> There is no sorrow so deep, God cannot soothe it"

Remember that the Lord is with us. (Isaiah 41:10) "Fear thou not; for I am with thee: be not dismayed; for I am thy God: I will strengthen thee; yea, I will help thee; yea, I will uphold thee with the right hand of my righteousness."

Only be thou strong and don't lost sight. (Joshua 1:7) "Only be thou strong and very courageous, that thou mayest observe to do according to all the law, which Moses my servant commanded thee: turn not from it to the right hand or to the left, that thou mayest prosper whithersoever thou goest." *Read your Bible and Pray and keep on praying until you're encouraged and challenged by the Lord and His Word.* (Acts 6:4) "But we will give ourselves continually to prayer, and to the ministry of the word." *Wait in the Lord and wait patiently.* (Isaiah 40:31) "But they that wait upon the LORD shall renew their strength; they shall mount up with wings as eagles; they shall run, and not be weary; and they shall walk, and not faint."

SUNDAY- MI DAILY DEVOTION
(I Samuel 30:6)

THE NEGATIVE EFFECTS OF DISCOURAGEMENT

6- "And David was greatly distressed; for the people spake of stoning him, because the soul of all the people was grieved, every man for his sons and for his daughters: but David encouraged himself in the LORD his God."

David exercised *CATHARSIS THERAPY* when he was under stressed.

Catharsis

"In other schools of psychotherapy, catharsis refers to the therapeutic release of emotions and tensions, although not necessarily unconscious ones such as Freud emphasized. Certain types of therapy in particular, such as psychodrama and primal scream therapy, have stressed the healing potential of cathartic experiences." (Taken from Healthline on the Internet)

Ca·thar·sis - kə-'thär-səs

"Etymology: New Latin, from Greek *katharsis,* from *kathairein* to cleanse, purge, from *katharos*

1: purgation

2 a: purification or purgation of the emotions (as pity and fear) primarily through art **b:** a purification or purgation that brings about spiritual renewal or release from tension

3 c: elimination of a complex by bringing it to consciousness and affording it expression" (Merriam-Webster Dictionary, Internet)

You will end up a loser if you are discouraged and you don't recognize your discouragement or if you don't take a step to get rid of it. You will be *distressed, disillusioned, disturbed, depressed and defeated.*

Satan is a defeated foe, but he never showed the whole world that he's been defeated at Calvary two thousand years ago. My personal belief, it was actually since God cast him and his angels out from Heaven and in the Garden of Eden. (Genesis 3: 15). He (Satan) will never win, but sometimes, it seems that some of the children of God, the children of the King of kings and Lord of lords are so discouraged and are living a defeated life. Don't let discouragement put you down and don't let it pull you down. Don't let Satan use discouragement to keep you away from God, God's Word, worship and ministry. Please meditate on these very common verses for every believers of the Lord Jesus Christ. Paul's great words of encouragement for us Christians in (Romans 8:28; 31-32) "And we know that all things work together for good to them that love God, to them who are the called according to his purpose. 31- What shall we then say to these things? If God be for us, who can be against us? 32- He that spared not his own Son, but delivered him up for us all, how shall he not with him also freely give us all things?"

MONDAY- MI DAILY DEVOTION
(Matthew 10:26-28)

HELL IS A PLACE OF NO MORE...

26- "Fear them not therefore: for there is nothing covered, that shall not be revealed; and hid, that shall not be known. 27- What I tell you in darkness, that speak ye in light: and what ye hear in the ear, that preach ye upon the housetops. 28- And fear not them which kill the body, but are not able to kill the soul: but rather fear him which is able to destroy both soul and body in hell."

Preaching about hell is a very sensitive topic to many pastors, preachers and churches. Some preachers won't preach about this subject for fear of setbacks from some of the members of their congregation. Also, for fear as someone may get offended on the subject. During the 80's and the 90's, open field evangelistic crusade with Christian movies on a big screen was so common in the Philippines. At one occasion, I was invited to speak in one of the crusade, where on its first part was the showing of the movie "The Burning Hell" by Estus Pirkle. While I was relaxing and praying and I was watching the movie, an individual approached me and told me that the pastor's idea (he was referring to the host pastor) of showing such movie was not a good idea. So, I asked him: "What made you say that?" He said, "Because, he is scaring the people, especially the children in showing this movie about hell." People sometimes will think that way, when you preach about hell, they thought you're scaring them so they will accept Christ as their Lord and Savior. Or they may think that you're trying to proselyte them in Christian religion or beliefs. Hell in the Bible is not a symbol or a picture of something in relation to earthly pain or suffering. And it's not just an experience or feeling. Hell is a real place with real people and a real punishment for those who reject the love of God and the gospel of the Lord Jesus Christ. (John 3: 16; 36; Luke 16:19- 31) Jesus himself preached about hell. In (Mark 9:45- 47) 45- "And if thy foot offend thee, cut it off: it is better for thee to enter halt into life, than having two feet to be cast into hell, into the fire that never shall be quenched: 46- Where their worm dieth not, and the fire is not quenched. 47- And if thine eye offend thee, pluck it out: it is better for thee to enter into the kingdom of God with one eye, than having two eyes to be cast into hell fire:" Jesus gave us a good picture of hell in those verses. The term hell in its common usage in the Scriptures designates to future punishment to the wicked, to those who will reject the Lord and Savior Jesus Christ. In hell: there will be no more love, no more care, no more forgiveness, no more peace, no more rest and no more joy.

In physical sense, in hell there will be no more family, no more worship, no more singing, no chance and second chance. Hell is a place of no more in a negative sense. It's the opposite of Heaven. In Heaven: there will be no more hate, no more careless people, no more war, no more sorrow and pain, no more bills to pay and no more tears and hunger and thirst. God loves us that He gave us His one and only Son so He can save us from the punishment of our sins. (John 3:36) "He that believeth on the Son hath everlasting life: and he that believeth not the Son shall not see life; but the wrath of God abideth on him."

TUESDAY- MI DAILY DEVOTION
(Mark 12: 41-44)

"SHE GAVE ALL THAT SHE HAD"

43- "And he called unto him his disciples, and saith unto them, Verily I say unto you, That this poor widow hath cast more in, than all they which have cast into the treasury: 44- For all they did cast in of their abundance; but she of her want did cast in all that she had, even all her living."

The comfort of the Widow… She knew that the Lord was there observing, 1- how the people gave, in verse 41 "…and beheld how the people cast money into the treasury:" People give with different reasons or purpose… (II Cor. 9:7) "Every man according as he purposeth in his heart, so let him give; not grudgingly, or of necessity: for God loveth a cheerful giver." The woman did not give from her huge bank account or from the top of her purse, but from the bottom of her heart. Giving should start from your heart. If you really want to be a generous person, don't wait for the time where you get a raised, you will become wealthy or don't wait 'till you win millions of dollars from the lottery. Don't even wait for that time where you are financially stable. You can start your generosity with your wife and children by giving them your time. Start from the bottom of your heart and from the bottom of your pocket and bank account. You just have to change your heart, change your purpose, change your perspective and change the way you love the Lord. Change the way you look at others. Start being a winner for God with the little amount that you can share or give in your church, for the ministry and for God's glory. *The Lord was there observing how much they gave, verse 43.* D.L.

Moody- "Do all the good you can, to all the people you can, in all the ways you can, as long as you can." Jesus was there watching on how much they gave, not because He was interested with money or with their money, but because He was interested on how much they express their love for Him through their giving. "GIVE 'TILL IT HURTS." Rabbi Harold Kushner-

"The purpose of life is not to win; the purpose of life is to grow and to share." *The Lord was there observing the way they gave.* Proper perspective and way of giving are: 1)-Give your heart to God for giving. 2)-Be open to the people who are in needs and be generous to the needy. 3)-Open your heart to God and let God open your purse to give. 4)-Praise God and don't expect anything in return. Remember to always give God the glory. (Matthew 6:2-4)

The commitment of the Widow... Larry Burkett, "Where there is no giving, there is no commitment." "The poor widow has put in more..."She gave all that she had in spite of her needs, her wants and in spite of her poverty. She gave to Jesus her whole livelihood and savings. That could be her last pay check, but she gave all of them anyways. *The commendation of Jesus...*1- The Lord commended her for her right attitude in giving. 2- The Lord commended her for her love for God. 3- The Lord commended her for pleasing the Lord in her poverty.

WEDNESDAY- MI DAILY DEVOTION
(Philippians 4:12-14)

MY SECRET THAT ONLY GOD AND MY WIFE KNOWS...

"I know both how to be abased, and I know how to abound: every where and in all things I am instructed both to be full and to be hungry, both to abound and to suffer need. 13- I can do all things through Christ which strengtheneth me. 14- Notwithstanding ye have well done, that ye did communicate with my affliction."

I was in Bacolod City with my family weeks before the catastrophic eruption of Mount Pinatubo in Zambales, Philippines in 1991. We went there to start a new church plant. But the president of our mission board asked me to go to Subic to help a pastor less church of which, I don't buy his idea, but we went anyways. First- I wanted to submit to my superior. Secondly- I wanted to give it a try. Thirdly- I kept the door open to possibilities and God given opportunities to serve in any capacity. And last, I was just taking a detour. So, we went back to Manila first, then to Bulacan, before *I* went to Subic. During those times, Subic, Zambales was the most dangerous place in the world. *I* took a bus going to Olongapo City and walked from Olongapo City to Subic City for three reasons: 1) the bus stops only in Olongapo City and they don't take trips to Subic as they used to due to lahars and some of the roads are not passable. 2) No public transportations such as jeepneys, taxi, bus or tricycle. 3) I did not have money to rent a car going to Subic. There's no option, but to walk in the mountainous and zigzag road for at least 10 miles. It was not as exciting as many Pastors have experienced on their journey to their new horizon and ministry. There was no welcome party, no dinner with the leaders and deacons, no new pastor's first Sunday celebration and no picking up from the airport. It was not a time of rejoicing or complaints, but it was a time for God's service. Dangers, discouragement, disappointments, hopelessness and death to some of the people and their friends and love ones were the sound of music at the moment. There was no children singing- "Oh, how He loves you and me…" or "Jesus loves me this I know, for the Bible tells me so…"

A day before I arrived, the church and its parsonage collapsed and were leveled to the ground due to the heavy ash fall with rains that fell on its roofs. The pulpit and a small karaoke machine were the only things left standing. Just imagine yourself coming to your new assignment with the news that almost 90% of your members whom you have never met yet have left the place. And you're stepping into the doors of the church and the parsonage with nothing but broken cabinets, G.I. sheets all over the place, broken beams and foundations, wet song books and Bibles, broken musical instruments, broken utensils and a dirty, smelly kitchen. And it's your first day in your new church and ministry. *Excitement* will not be the word. Joy and dreams could not be possible in the human eye. Good planning, goals and great visions will not fit in our present situations at that time. All you hear during those times were deaths, injuries, collapsing of homes and buildings, complains, hopelessness, questions and pointing of finger against heaven. The first day I saw the place as I took the tour to personally see the damaged and devastation, it was unbelievable! I was walking along Calapandayan, where all the night clubs and the strip clubs are and I felt like God has turned His back from the place. You see people crying and waiting for mercy and help!

And I felt like the glory of God has departed- "Icabod". I felt like God's finger was pointing to the place with judgment in His hands. I felt like looking at the face of God with mixed emotions of anger, love, judgment and sorrow for their sins. My only desire during those times was recovery. My only comfort was I know God was with me and I know I'm going to make it by God's grace and in the strength of the Lord.

After the eruption of Mount Pinatubo, we started building the chapel from the ash fall as we made hollow blocks out of it. God replaced the chapel from a small wooden bamboo church building to a bigger and designed for 2 stories concrete chapel. I did not tell anyone about what I felt and the not so pleasant experiences I had until the day I write this portion. It was only God and my wife who knows what I felt and the physical, emotional and spiritual struggles I had. But we have the assurance of God's perfect time, God's love and His hand upon us. I hope that these verses from Apostle Paul's writings will encourage us all. (Romans 8:28; 36- 39) "And we know that all things work together for good to them that love God, to them who are the called according to his purpose. 36- As it is written, For thy sake we are killed all the day long; we are accounted as sheep for the slaughter. 37- Nay, in all these things we are more than conquerors through him that loved us. 38- For I am persuaded, that neither death, nor life, nor angels, nor principalities, nor powers, nor things present, nor things to come, 39- Nor height, nor depth, nor any other creature, shall be able to separate us from the love of God, which is in Christ Jesus our Lord."

THURSDAY- MI DAILY DEVOTION
(Ephesians 5:2; 21-25)

"MY MARRIAGE IS A LOVE TRIANGLE"

21- "And walk in love, as Christ also hath loved us, and hath given himself for us an offering and a sacrifice to God for a sweetsmelling savour."

Friends and brethren remember that marriage is God's divine institution. In an introduction to a wedding ceremony, a pastor would usually say: "Friends and brethren, we are gathered here today, to unite this man and this woman in holy matrimony. Marriage was first instituted by God in the garden of Eden, when He saw that it is not good for a man to be alone. Even the Apostle Paul crowned marriage when He compared it to Christ's relationship with the church. That's the reason why we entered marriage with care, love and honor to God and to each other. The Bible said, 'For this cause shall a man leave his father and mother, and shall be joined unto his wife, and they two shall be one flesh'." (Hebrews 13:4) "Marriage is honourable in all, and the bed undefiled: but whoremongers and adulterers God will judge." (Proverbs 18:22) You find favour of the Lord when you get married. You don't make fun or take marriage lightly. When you enter marriage, you're entering into a bonding or vow that was made in Heaven. The vow is between you, your spouse and the Lord. Your relationship with your partner is way more important than anyone and more important than any relationship in the world. It's more important than anything in the world; including money, sports, friends and even your ministry. Your family and your relationship with your spouse should come first. You really have to try hard and harder as you try to maintain your loving and sacrificial love relationship with your spouse; because marriage is inspired and blessed by God. God was the author of marriage and He was the one who married the first couple which was in the garden of Eden when God tie the knots between Adam and Eve. In your relationship, God will come first and then your spouse next... There is no such thing as hard or easy marriage or partner. When you get married, whatever is hard for you and your partner will be easy if you love one another and the two of you love the Lord your God. And it should start by knowing Christ as your Lord and Savior.

Here is a simple guide on how to know Christ as your Lord and Savior: **Accept**: Accept that you are a sinner before God. (Romans. 3: 10; 23, 6: 23). Accept that He (Jesus) alone can forgive your sins and trespasses. And accept Him as your Savior and Lord of your life. **Believe**: Believe on the Lord Jesus Christ as your Savior and Lord. Believe that Jesus Died for your sins on the cross and he was buried and after 3 days was rose from the dead. (Romans 10: 6- 13, John 1: 12). **Confess**: Confess your sins before God. You ask the Lord to forgive you of your sins and to cleanse you. (I John 1: 8- 10, Acts 3: 19, 8: 22, II Peter 3:9) And as you decide to ask Jesus to come into your heart, you pray this prayer sincerely and seriously: "Dear God and Heavenly Father; I know, I am a sinner. Please forgive me of my sins and cleanse me with your Precious Blood. I now invite you Lord Jesus to come into my heart. By faith, I now accept you as my personal Lord and Savior of my life, In Jesus Name. Amen!"

FRIDAY- MI DAILY DEVOTION
(John 2:1-11)

THE WEDDING AT CANA AND THE MIRACLE OF JESUS

"And the third "day there was a marriage in Cana of Galilee; and the mother of Jesus was there: 2- And both Jesus was called, and his disciples, to the marriage. 3- And when they wanted wine, the mother of Jesus saith unto him, They have no wine. 4- Jesus saith unto her, Woman, what have I to do with thee? mine hour is not yet come. 5- His mother saith unto the servants, Whatsoever he saith unto you, do it. 6- And there were set there six waterpots of stone, after the manner of the purifying of the Jews, containing two or three firkins apiece. 7- Jesus saith unto them, Fill the waterpots with water. And they filled them up to the brim. 8- And he saith unto them, Draw out now, and bear unto the governor of the feast. And they bare it. 9- When the ruler of the feast had tasted the water that was made wine, and knew not whence it was: (but the servants which drew the water knew;) the governor of the feast called the bridegroom, 10- And saith unto him, Every man at the beginning doth set forth good wine; and when men have well drunk, then that which is worse: but thou hast kept the good wine until now. 11- This beginning of miracles did Jesus in Cana of Galilee, and manifested forth his glory; and his disciples believed on him."

When Jesus started His public ministry, His first miracle was performed at the marriage in Cana of Galilee. Wedding or marriage has a special place in the heart of the Lord Jesus Christ. He gave importance to marriage by attending, providing and even performing such miracle. The Lord's miracle indicates how our lives have changed. He changed the water into wine. This blessing of eternal life received by faith is seen in the water turned into wine at Cana, near Nazareth in Galilee. It's a picture of God's mighty works in the heart of man. The first sign or miracle of Christ shows us that He is the giver of life and that He is able to change water into wine. God can change the life that has no flavor and color into something that is enjoyable or full of love and joy. He can make and show us miracles in our marriage. He can make miracles in our colorless or in the dark room of our life. The Creator alone can be our spiritual Re-creator. He alone can give us the best wine which cannot make you an alcoholic but gives us a joyous life. (Isaiah 55:1; Ephesians 5:18-20). "Ho, every one that thirsteth, come ye to the waters, and he that hath no money; come ye, buy, and eat; yea, come, buy wine and milk without money and without price."

It's a great blessing to know that the Lord's first miracle as He starts His public ministry happened in a marriage in Cana. It would mean to me that God: 1- Honors the marriage between a man and a woman. 2- God's blessings are on a marriage couples or in a family. 3- God is interested in a wedding, in a marriage relationship based on His Word, or in a family with a man (the husband, father or head of the family) and a woman (the wife, mother or housewife).

Paul revealed a great truth about this mystery in (Ephesians 5:22-23; 32) "Wives, submit yourselves unto your own husbands, as unto the Lord. 23- For the husband is the head of the wife, even as Christ is the head of the church: and he is the saviour of the body. 32- This is a great mystery: but I speak concerning Christ and the church."

41

SATURDAY- MI DAILY DEVOTION
(Ephesians 5:25-31)

WHY MARRIAGE *IS NOT*...

25- "Husbands, love your wives, even as Christ also loved the church, and gave himself for it; 26- That he might sanctify and cleanse it with the washing of water by the word, 27- That he might present it to himself a glorious church, not having spot, or wrinkle, or any such thing; but that it should be holy and without blemish. 28- So ought men to love their wives as their own bodies. He that loveth his wife loveth himself. 29- For no man ever yet hated his own flesh; but nourisheth and cherisheth it, even as the Lord the church: 30- For we are members of his body, of his flesh, and of his bones. 31- For this cause shall a man leave his father and mother, and shall be joined unto his wife, and they two shall be one flesh."

What *IS NOT* in marriage? Married couples should know how to take care of their relationship and their home. I believe in mixed marriages, but I don't agree with same sex marriage. It's not Biblical, moral and it's very inappropriate. So marriage *IS NOT* for same sex, but for opposite sex. Marriage *IS NOT* for trial and error. Marriage *IS NOT* like a song- "Que sera, sera; whatever will be, will be". Marriage *IS NOT* a temporary commitment, but a lifetime commitment. Marriage *IS NOT* a "ninety days return policy", marriage is *NO RETURN, NO EXCHANGE* policy. Whether you like him/her or not after the honeymoon, you have to keep him/her in spite of his/her attitude. He/she might be your worst nightmare after that Hollywood like honeymoon in Hawaii or Bahamas. You have to give him/her a try for another months or years. Have you ever thought of this before you step on that sanctuary to give your vows to each other or when you were on the seashore during your honeymoon, while you're holding his/her hand...? That one day there will be baby's crying in the middle of the night and that baby needs milk and clothes to put on. And that little cute and adorable baby one day will go to college and will not obey or listen to you and... there will be bills to pay? Marriage *IS NOT* an experiment and *IS NOT* for experiment. There is church wedding and garden wedding, but there's no such thing as wedding and marriage laboratory where you can be a scientist of your own and do an experiment with your relationship and your marriage. I'm not always happy with my marriage because we have conflicts and misunderstanding, but I love my children and I have to love my wife. I have fun with them and enjoy watching them grow, but I don't take marriage lightly and don't make fun of it. Marriage is a serious matter. It was God who made marriage. It's either you will learn to love or not to love at all. If you get married outside of God's will and without 'LOVE', that marriage will never work. I don't have a perfect marriage because I don't have a perfect partner. I only have a godly wife and a mother. I don't like everything I see, I've heard, I know... with my wife, but that's how I've learned to love her more and more. Marriage *IS NOT* all about YOU. If marriage is all about YOU, then you don't need a wife/husband, but a machine or a servant, so you can use them and make them do everything and at any time in your own disposal. Marriage *IS NOT* just about sex, but *commitment, cooperation, communication* and most of all pleasing Christ. Please read and meditate together on Peter's advice to us as couples... (I Peter 3:1- 8) 1- "Likewise, ye wives, be in subjection to your own husbands; that, if any obey not the word, they also may without the word be won by the conversation of the wives; 2- While they behold your chaste conversation coupled with fear. 3- Whose adorning let it not be that outward adorning of plaiting the hair, and of wearing of gold, or of putting on of apparel; 4- But let it be the hidden man of the heart, in that which is not corruptible, even the ornament of a meek and quiet spirit, which is in the sight of God of great price. 5- For after this manner in the old time the holy women also, who trusted in God, adorned themselves, being in subjection unto their own husbands: 6- Even as Sara obeyed Abraham, calling him lord: whose daughters ye are, as long as ye do well, and are not afraid with any amazement. 7- Likewise, ye husbands, dwell with them according to knowledge, giving honour unto the wife, as unto the weaker vessel, and as being heirs together of the grace of life; that your prayers be not hindered. 8- Finally, be ye all of one mind, having compassion one of another, love as brethren, be pitiful, be courteous:"

SUNDAY- MI DAILY DEVOTION
(Philippians 1:7-11)

MISSION TRIPS HURDLES...

7- "Even as "it is meet for me to think this of you all, because I have you in my heart; inasmuch as both in my bonds, and in the defence and confirmation of the gospel, ye all are partakers of my grace. 8- For God is my record, how greatly I long after you all in the bowels of Jesus Christ. 9- And this I pray, that your love may abound yet more and more in knowledge and in all judgment; 10- That ye may approve things that are excellent; that ye may be sincere and without offence till the day of Christ; 11- Being filled with the fruits of righteousness, which are by Jesus Christ, unto the glory and praise of God."

At the time of this writing, we are in Miami International Airport (MIA) waiting for our flight to Detroit from Belize and Guatemala trips. I am travelling with Mario and Nico Merginio together with my son Eliezer and daughter Eliel Lyn and our youth member and photographer Paul John Farinas. The Lord has blessed our first international mission trip as a team and a church. It was a very tiring and stressful preparation, but a very fruitful trip. We did garage sales, and I took pictures and framed them and sell them or some were for donations which did not do much. It was a worthwhile investment and cause. Some people give more than expected and I praise the Lord for them. Let me say thank you to all who supported this cause and only eternity will tell how you have touched lives from home with your prayers and financial support. I also would like to thank my very supportive and missions minded and mission focus members who sacrificed and gave their time, shared their love and gave in so many ways to support this cause and God's heartbeat and passions to make this endeavor happen for God's Kingdom and glory. The very day we left early in the morning at about 4:00 AM; I felt already that something will not go right and some problems will arise. And I was right, although in my mind, I tried to have a positive mind set, still problem comes up in which I thought would really be costly to 4 of us. We flew American Airlines from Detroit to Miami, but when we were in Miami; our names were not on the master list on our scheduled flight to Belize. The only way we could fly that day was for us to pay $159.00 each. On our schedule, our flight was supposed to be Detroit to Miami, Florida on the 19th and then we were scheduled to fly to Belize on the 20th which means that we have to sleep over night in Miami airport or in a hotel if we decide not to pay the changed of schedule or flight. At that time, it was already 10:30 AM and we would have to walk passing about 20 to 25 gates to the customer service and then we will have to wait for the supervisor to come after knowing that the lady on the counter can't do anything about our issues. And it took about 20 to 30 minutes for the supervisor to get to the counter where we were waiting to settle our problems. Another bad news and stressful situation was, the supervisor of the American Airlines told us to go back down to the baggage claim and pick up our baggage and then go to the ticket counter and see *IF* they will let us fly without any extra charges. I have tried to explained and convinced the supervisor including telling her that the kids don't have the money and we're running out of time since our flight would be at around 12:30 at noon. And to make the long story short, we went to the baggage claim area and found our luggage just about to be taken to the office for storage. When I think about the hassle and the pain and stress of going back and forth and trying to race with time because we only have 45 minutes left to board, I dropped my luggage and in my mind I said, "I think we will just have to fly the next day and just enjoy our time while we are in Miami, Florida. After a while, a very courteous gentleman from American Airlines asked me if I need help. And I said, "Yes Sir…" He ask me to come down and at the same time push his lady co-worker off the computer, so he could use the computer in which really made that lady mad and outraged. The other thing that you don't want to hear while you're under stress and really wanted to get into your plane was- "they're going to close the door in a minute or the door is closed already…" And those were the words of the other lady who happens to be so annoying to all of us. But by the grace of God, we were able to fly on the same plane. And when we were in Belize, the custom charged us $20.00 US dollars for the stuff we brought in which leads to an argument with the customs in Belize, but we end up paying anyways. And one of our bags got lost. Of course we wanted to abide by the law of the land, but we also have to be wise and not just do what they may want us to do without knowing the real issues. We made it again and we got our missing luggage the next day. Praise God for the *not so good* situations that we went through, because it tested our attitude and character. It shows the real YOU when you are in a situations like what we went through. I believe it's all because of God's grace and also, because of you who prayed and believe in what we are doing. We have the same desire, purpose, goal and focus which is Kingdom focus. Again, thank you so much and we really appreciate your desire to be used by God in some ways even by sharing your wealth and blessings. God bless you all!!!

MONDAY- MI DAILY DEVOTION
(I Corinthians 15:58)

MISSION TRIPS FIRST SET OF VICTORY

"Therefore, my beloved brethren, be ye stedfast, unmoveable, always abounding in the work of the Lord, forasmuch as ye know that your labour is not in vain in the Lord."

I don't really know which part is the first set of victory in our mission trips to Belize and Guatemala. Some of the people from all parts of the world including people from the United States of America go to these places for Vacation and pleasures. But it was different for our team and our church. We went there to make a difference and to reach out and help churches and tell others about Jesus. But I believe that the first set of victory was when we presented the cause to our church and we all agreed in unity, with the same mind, with the same heart, with the same passion and the same purpose in the Lord and for His glory. If you would talk about emotional or spiritual hurdles, it's having the right heart and the right attitudes when we found out that some of us needed a Visa to go to Belize and Guatemala. If it's about money, finances or fund raising, it was when we were about 5 weeks before the scheduled trip and we only have more than $40.00 US dollars and few Canadian dollars in our bucket and we needed more than $4,000 US dollars as fees for the mission organization in a matter of days. If you would talk about the outcome of our stay… the first set of victory could be when we were in our first day in Belize and we already built a good and healthy relationship with the staff of the mission organization. If you would talk about helping the churches; I believe it was on our second day in

Guatemala after the preaching of Reverend Mario Merginio. We have 2 professions of faith. Actually, on our first night of worship in a Guatemalan church, the Lord moved in a special way and we felt His presence. We always have the victory if we're doing the Lord's work. No matter where we are and what we do, as long as we're doing it heartily and for the glory of our God. It should always be a blessing and a victory that we can share and offered in the throne of glory. My mind was set up already when we were getting ready for this trip. I was thinking already of being a blessing and that God would use me and the group to be a blessing to this group of people, but it did not work that way, but it was the other way around. On our first night in a small congregation in Guatemala, I was convicted and was touched by the Holy Spirit of God, when I saw the Spirit working in the lives of the Christians back there and how God has worked in their worship that night. The almost 4 hours of worship and singing praises to our God seems to be so short if the Holy Spirit is at work. Or the first set of victory could be this letter from Eliezer D. Sagansay: "Firstly, I would like to thank you for being a part of our mission trip to Belize and Guatemala. God did some amazing things in Belize and Guatemala. We spent 4 days serving in Guatemala. We thank God for giving us the opportunity to serve the church in Guatemala. For many years, the church has been meeting in homes. However, their vision was to have their own church building. Four years ago, the church decided to sell fast food items such as tacos and enchiladas, to raise funds for their church building. We were very encouraged by their love for Jesus and their heart to continue the work of God in Guatemala. We brought $1000 worth of paint in Guatemala to help them out and they were very happy that God has provided. We also wanted to bless their pastor and we bought him $150 worth of groceries (this is a cartful in

Guatemala). We also handed out hygiene items, candies, Gospel tracts, and toys to the children. We praise God because He provides for our needs. He begins a good work and completes it! (Philippians 1:26).

In Belize, we served the community by painting a house owned by a former gang leader. Please pray for his salvation. We also had the opportunity to meet kids in an orphanage and interact with them. Pastor Mark Humes our guide and the man who wears so many hats and Jose Antonio our interpreter were such a great blessing to all of us. They are very patient and helpful to us.

There are so many things that I would like to say; but letters, pictures, and videos could not express them. Our mission trip to Belize and Guatemala has been a life-changing experienced. I know that God will continue His work in us and through us. Thank you for your prayers and your support!"

TUESDAY- MI DAILY DEVOTION
(Psalms 69:16-20)

THE SECOND SETS OF VICTORY AND BLESSINGS

16- "Hear me, O LORD; for thy lovingkindness is good: turn unto me according to the multitude of thy tender mercies. 17- And hide not thy face from thy servant; for I am in trouble: hear me speedily. 18- Draw nigh unto my soul, and redeem it: deliver me because of mine enemies. 19- Thou hast known my reproach, and my shame, and my dishonour: mine adversaries are all before thee. 20- Reproach hath broken my heart; and I am full of heaviness: and I looked for some to take pity, but there was none; and for comforters, but I found none."

The first time we met the pastor of a small congregation in Guatemala, he was not very accommodating to us. I fully agree with what one of our team said which is very understandable, he was kind of shy. He can't understand and speak English, so what would you expect. But on the other side of the coin, the Lord was putting the burden to our host, tour guide and supervisor. He is very humble, sensitive especially with the condition and needs of the people and the pastor. There's no doubt that it was the Lord who placed it in his heart, as he shared to us the economic or financial conditions of the Guatemalan pastor.

I believe that one of the victories that we experienced was the two professions of faith and the blessing of watching those who received the tracts and read them during our tracts distribution on Sunday afternoon. But, also one of the very dramatic experienced that we have in Guatemala was when pastor Mark decided to change the itinerary from us continuing painting the church to just go with him and visit the pastor's house. So Mario and Paul John Farinas who took pictures and video went with us while Eliezer, Nico and Eliel Lyn stayed at the church finishing the painting. The pastor of the church toured us to his very small house. I can't picture to you and say or express it in words about the housing condition of the pastor. In my almost 30 years in the ministry, I've never seen one like that. It breaks my heart that it was like a nightmare for me just to think of his financial condition and of just thinking of the house where he and his family lived in. The pastor was receiving 400 quetzal which would just be about $75.00 US dollars a month. Sometimes, if the giving were down, he would just end up with $50.00 or less. I honestly cried several times, every time I remember his poor state. At the time of this writing, I cried and my heart breaks about the hardships that this man of God is going through. We prayed under his roof and we tried to encouraged and comfort him and while we were praying and asking God to bless him and pour down His blessing upon them, it started to rain and it poured out really hard and I felt some water dropping on my head and my hand from this man's roof. And just like what Eliezer mentioned in his letter, we took him to the grocery store and told him to get anything he wants and needs. At first, the pastor just took some detergents and a gallon of bleach, bath soaps and toothpaste. I did not see all those necessities in his house when we were there. And I believe that that could be the reason why he picked up what he needed the most and rushed to the cashier thinking that we were done shopping already. I tried to make him comfortable by letting him know that were more than willing to pay for whatever he needs. And I was surprised when I heard his daughter whispering to him in Spanish in which I know was…, "Dad, get some apple please…" When I asked her, "Do you want some apple?" she said, "Si Senor, por pabor…" "Yes Sir, Please…" She took one of the apples and she was surprised when I gave her 10 apples. She was surprised when she just wanted a piece of hot dog and I gave her 2 packs of hot dogs and some turkey ham.

We have those people who love the Lord and serve the Lord faithfully, but they don't have enough. I hope and pray that you could be a part of what God is doing in us and through us. We will try to help this pastor not just in prayer, but also financially. Please help us as we touch lives and make a difference. We are also praying that the Lord will open the door for this pastor to be able to come here in the States. God Bless us all and TO GOD BE THE GLORY!!!

WEDNESDAY- MI DAILY DEVOTION
(Matthew 6:1-6)

"BE YOURSELF... KEEPIN' IT REAL..."

1- "Take heed that ye do not your alms before men, to be seen of them: otherwise ye have no reward of your Father which is in heaven. 2- Therefore when thou doest thine alms, do not sound a trumpet before thee, as the hypocrites do in the synagogues and in the streets, that they may have glory of men. Verily I say unto you, They have their reward. 3- But when thou doest alms, let not thy left hand know what thy right hand doeth: 4- That thine alms may be in secret: and thy Father which seeth in secret himself shall reward thee openly. 5- And when thou prayest, thou shalt not be as the hypocrites are: for they love to pray standing in the synagogues and in the corners of the streets, that they may be seen of men. Verily I say unto you, They have their reward. 6- But thou, when thou prayest, enter into thy closet, and when thou hast shut thy door, pray to thy Father which is in secret; and thy Father which seeth in secret shall reward thee openly."

How can you be a blessing to others? Making a good comments and good words or remarks should come along with good works. We can be a good motivational speaker or a good encourager, but we can't be as effective as *if* we live the Word. Have you heard of the three faces of "the present day publicans"? I believe your answer could be... "No, not yet..." Or you may have something different in mind. The three faces of "the present day publicans" would be: 1- His face is different when he's at home; 2- His face is different when he's at work 3- And his face is different when he's at church. This is the kind of man or woman you see at home, at work or at church. People sometimes would act like a man with an iron mask. Do you know that some people are like that, behind that iron masks is a different person. You only see the mask, but not the real face of a person behind the masks. Some Christians can mask themselves even in their giving. (Matthew 6:1-2) It is very obvious to people who gave to charity for personal interests. It always depends on how an individual gave… you can give with something in mind beside from doing it out of love and for the glory of God as what Jesus said in verses 3 and 4. A Christian can also masks himself even in his prayer. Prayer is talking to God and it means that you are coming to the throne of grace and you don't take it lightly. I remember when we were in a small church in Guatemala where the members, especially the leaders would come in into the church and go straight to the altar to kneel down and pray before the worship service starts. We should have the same attitude and practice. We come to church with an earnest desire and eagerness to worship and pray. No wonder that a small congregation can really worship the Lord and you can really feel the presence of God in their worship. Check out what Jesus said in the Book of (Matthew 6:5-6) "And when thou prayest, thou shalt not be as the hypocrites are: for they love to pray standing in the Synagogues and in the corners of the streets, that they may be seen of men. Verily I say unto you, They have their reward. 6- But thou, when thou prayest, enter into thy closet, and when thou hast shut thy door, pray to thy Father which is in secret; and thy Father which seeth in secret shall reward thee openly."

THURSDAY- MI DAILY DEVOTION
(Genesis 2:7-8)

RELATIONSHIP- ETERNAL AND SO BASIC

7- "And the LORD God formed man of the dust of the ground, and breathed into his nostrils the breath of life; and man became a living soul. 8- And the LORD God planted a garden eastward in Eden; and there he put the man whom he had formed."

When God created man and placed them in the garden of Eden…, He created man with a purpose and something unique and special in His mind. (Genesis 1:25-27) When God created us, He created us with His own hand, while He created everything else with His Words.

When God created the whole universe, He just spoke the words and everything just came into order like it was engineered and well planned for millions of years and by billions of people in which could not be possible for men to do. But God in His power made all things possible. How many of us people have ever thought of God's amazing hands and personal touched in His creation, specifically the human beings. The Master's touched on the day He created man was a sign and a proof that God wants to have a love relationship with us. When Adam and Eve sinned, God Himself made an offering for the cleansing and restoration of the broken relationship and a marred love relationship between God and man. God killed an animal and shed its blood as a picture of Christ's death on the Cross.

I believe that the true foundation of the true religion is God in the person of the Lord Jesus Christ who took our sins on the Cross. He is the one who saved us to the uttermost. (Hebrews 7:22-27) "By so much was Jesus made a surety of a better testament. 23- And they truly were many priests, because they were not suffered to continue by reason of death: 24- But this man, because he continueth ever, hath an unchangeable priesthood. 25- Wherefore he is able also to save them to the uttermost that come unto God by him, seeing he ever liveth to make intercession for them. 26- For such an high priest became us, who is holy, harmless, undefiled, separate from sinners, and made higher than the heavens; 27- Who needeth not daily, as those high priests, to offer up sacrifice, first for his own sins, and then for the people's: for this he did once, when he offered up himself." The word "uttermost" in verse 25 means "completely" or "perfectly". It is true that Christ can save you and me completely and perfectly by His grace through faith and repentance. And it is where the Basic and eternal relationship with the eternal God will start. It is by putting your trust to the founder and true foundation of a true religion- our Savior and Lord. If you do that: Jesus will save you to the uttermost, it means from your sins, from Satan, from your selfishness, from the punishment of Hell, from hopelessness and you can just name it… the Bible said in (Ephesians 2:8-10) "For by grace are ye saved through faith; and that not of yourselves: it is the gift of God: 9- Not of works, lest any man should boast. 10- For we are his workmanship, created in Christ Jesus unto good works, which God hath before ordained that we should walk in them."

FRIDAY- MI DAILY DEVOTION
(Mark 12:28-33)

LOVE RELATIONSHIPS IS THE ESSENTIAL

28- "And one of the scribes came, and having heard them reasoning together, and perceiving that he had answered them well, asked him, Which is the first commandment of all? 29- And Jesus answered him, The first of all the commandments is, Hear, O Israel; The Lord our God is one Lord: 30- And thou shalt love the Lord thy God with all thy heart, and with all thy soul, and with all thy mind, and with all thy strength: this is the first commandment. 31- And the second is like, namely this, Thou shalt love thy neighbour as thyself. There is none other commandment greater than these. 32- And the scribe said unto him, Well, Master, thou hast said the truth: for there is one God; and there is none other but he: 33- And to love him with all the heart, and with all the understanding, and with all the soul, and with all the strength, and to love his neighbour as himself, is more than all whole burnt offerings and sacrifices."

God wanted to have a love relationship with every man and woman all over the world. And it is indispensable or irreplaceable. He will not look at the color of your skin, your family background and not even your financial standing. He loves every individual, including those who are in the tribes and those who are in the uttermost parts of the earth. I remember the song that we used to sing in our Sunday school class when I was a little boy: "Jesus loves the little children, all the children of the world, Black and Yellow, Brown and White; All are precious in His sight; Jesus loves the little children of the world." Of course we know that

God loves the little children and the youths and adults as well. I believe that the most important thing in life is our relationships. As children of God, we should really take good care of our relationships with God, family and church or friends. We must start with God. Many, many, years ago I was wondering why (Deuteronomy 6:4-7) specifically verse 5 was mentioned by the Lord Jesus Christ as the first commandment. And then the more I grew in the Lord, the more I realized the real reasons. The Scriptures talks about loving God. If you will let me put the four verses together in one word, it would be- *PASSION*. Loving God should be our passion. Loving God must be from the inside out in our heart and it flows through our life. The passion within us which is in our soul is manifested in us and through us. It is in our whole being and in our practical theology. It should be in everything we do as Christians. You teach it and you testify about that love. You think about it even when you're taking some rests, in your bed and when you're at home in your free time. You think and take that passion with you and that love with you even in your business trips or on your vacation trips. You have that passion and love for God when you are in a mission trip. You think and have that passion for God and that love for God when you go to bed and as you get up in the morning. Here are some of the beautiful reminders for us from the man who really loves the Lord our God, his name is Moses. (Deuteronomy 6:15-17) 15- "(For the LORD thy God is a jealous God among you) lest the anger of the LORD thy God be kindled against thee, and destroy thee from off the face of the earth. 16- Ye shall not tempt the LORD your God, as ye tempted him in Massah. 17- Ye shall diligently keep the commandments of the LORD your God, and his testimonies, and his statutes, which he hath commanded thee."

SATURDAY- MI DAILY DEVOTION
(Luke 10:25-29)

MAINTAIN A HEALTHY RELATIONSHIP WITH YOUR FAMILY.

27- "And he answering said, Thou shalt love the Lord thy God with all thy heart, and with all thy soul, and with all thy strength, and with all thy mind; and thy neighbour as thyself."

What is more important to you? Have you ever asked yourself about your priorities concerning relationship? Next to God should be your family circle. Your relationship with your spouse is more important than any other relationships, it's next to God. It's so ironic to know of how many people would spend most of their time with friends and spend their leftovers to their family. Build that sweet and close relationship with your wife or husband and kids by spending time with them. If parents would only be at home for their kids; I believe we can keep our children away from drugs, violent and other crimes. If they see a father and a mother figure at home and they feel the love they needed at home, I don't think we would have problems with kids keeping them away from jail or vices. The Lord by His grace has blessed me with good kids, but it did not just come like a rain or sunshine when you get up in the morning. There was a price to be paid for which would be unconditional love, discipline, breaking of bad habits, teaching them and leading them to the Lord. You have to pay the price of *you* always being there for them. You have to support them and encourage them. *You* have to involve yourself in their dreams and talents. And sometimes you have to sacrifice with what you want for them and sacrifice your own principles and desire on their behalf. We may call it adjustment and I'm not talking about moral issues. Regarding your relationship with your spouse, you have to exercise the same principles. You have to love your wife. Husbands, you can always relate on this that the reason why Paul said: "Husbands, love your wives..." were: 1- Because God knows that husbands will always have problems with their wives. 2- The common problems of husbands to their wives are "submission and obedience." (Ephesians 5:25) And these are the same problems that we have with our relationship with Christ as a church. We always disobey and don't submit to God's Word and God's will for us. And if not for God's love and grace, we will all be lost and miserable. (Ephesians 5:21-23) And husbands would sometimes complain about their wives not being submissive and obedient, when we ourselves are not even submissive and obedient to God and His Word and will. The Lord wants for us to love our neighbors and your closes neighbors are those who lives under your roof. Verse 27 "And he answering said, Thou shalt love the Lord thy God with all thy heart, and with all thy soul, and with all thy strength, and with all thy mind; and thy neighbour as thyself." You have to love your neighbors even if you think they're not that cool. Your relationship with your spouse and kids is more important than anyone and anything in this world. Keep it up and be sure to maintain it. A great reminder for all of us is from the great Apostle Paul in the Book of (Ephesians 5:1-2; 33) "Be ye therefore followers of God, as dear children; 2- And walk in love, as Christ also hath loved us, and hath given himself for us an offering and a sacrifice to God for a sweetsmelling savour." 33- "Nevertheless let every one of you in particular so love his wife even as himself; and the wife see that she reverence her husband."

SUNDAY- MI DAILY DEVOTION
(Proverbs 27:17; 18:24; 17:17; 6:1)

LOVE YOUR FRIENDS AND KEEP THAT FRIENDSHIP...

27:17- "Iron sharpeneth iron; so a man sharpeneth the countenance of his friend."

18:24- "A man that hath friends must show himself friendly: and there is a friend that sticketh closer than a brother."

17:17- "A friend loveth at all times, and a brother is born for adversity."

6:1- "My son, if thou be surety for thy friend, if thou hast stricken thy hand with a stranger,"

Friendship will either make you or break you. As believers, we should take good care of our relationship with our friends and our relationship with our brethren in the Lord. We should love them, keep them in our prayers, support them in any way we can and just be there for them. "Iron sharpeneth iron;" It means that we need to communicate, share our wisdom and knowledge, care about them, share our ideas and be a comfort to our friends. A Christian should at least have a best friend in the body of Christ or in his/her home church to pray and fellowship with. And you should at least have someone whom you can trust to share your personal problems and confidential issues. And on the other end, we should be careful not to share any personal issues to others. Just a reminder for us who belongs in the body of Christ; we should maintain that love, trust, understanding and being open and available to our friends and brethren. I remember a good friend of mine telling me one day, he said: "Ely, don't lost a single friend… No matter what happened, just keep that friendship and keep it open." You may have heard of people who lost a friend because of non moral issues. The worst thing that can happen is when you lost a friend because of minor issues. There are issues or personal conflicts that you can just sleep over with or settle them over a cup of coffee.

"A true friend is a helper when you're helpless;

A true friend is a hope when you're hopeless,

A true friend is a wall to lean on when you're alone,

And the one whom you can lean on…
when no one is there for you…

A true friend is a shoulder to cry on when comfort
is gone… and betrayal is imminent.

A true friend is a present help in time of trouble.

A true friend is a bed to lie on when the
day is done and your sleep is gone;

A friend is a friend no matter what
and no matter where…

A friend will always be a friend." ElyRS.

A good example of true friendship and love for an enemy in the New Testament is in (Luke 10:30-37) which would be the story of Good Samaritan.

MONDAY- MI DAILY DEVOTION
(Matthew 28:19- 20)

TEACHING THEM MISSIONS…

19- "Go ye therefore, and teach all nations, baptizing them in the name of the Father, and of the Son, and of the Holy Ghost: 20- Teaching them to observe all things whatsoever I have commanded you: and, lo, I am with you alway, even unto the end of the world. Amen."

We have a family in our church who made the little shoe box, "the mission fund box" for their children to put their loose coins. They collect all the change they got from their parents and whenever they got a change back from the store or fast food restaurant. Mr. and Mrs. Gary Garcia cannot go out there for mission trips, especially their kids, but the Garcia's are teaching their children how to get involved in mission already. I really praise the Lord for Philippine International Christian Church where I am now their pastor for 3 years. They love missions, missionaries and supporting the mission work. Our church supports missionaries here in the United States of America and abroad. We shipped boxes (Balikbayan boxes) full of dry goods and other non perishable stuff to the Philippines for pastors, churches, schools and missionaries. We also send boxes of books and Bibles. We sent 7 people to Belize and Guatemala in 2010. Every time we have a visiting missionary or pastor, we don't let them leave empty and we don't let them go without a good amount of love gift and give them groceries, clothes or make them shop for free in our small missionary closet as our church calls it. We were told to "GO" and we must "GO." For the eleven disciples of the Lord Jesus Christ, it was really a divine appointment for them (verse 16). "Then the eleven disciples went …where Jesus had appointed them." And in (verse 17) "…they worshipped him: but some doubted." It was a divine appointment and worship, but others doubted. While in (verse 18) "And Jesus came and spake unto them, saying, All power is given unto me in heaven and in earth." It was a divine acknowledgment of the Lord Jesus Christ and of His Lordship. Here the Lord appointed His disciples to "Go and make disciples" and God appointed us to do the same. As Christians, we are responsible and duty bound to educate our children, the new converts and the church to get involved in mission. Let's make them involved in reaching out to the lost in anyways we can.

It's good to have transferred membership, but God will not ask us in heaven how many people transferred to our church for membership or how many people the church have proselytes. It's good to see a chapel or an auditorium full of people on ordinary Sundays, but if they're not saved, it would be like another organization or meeting. Our duty and responsibility is to win them to Christ. Many of those who church hopping may not even be a believer of the Lord Jesus Christ, so start winning them for Christ. (Acts 1:8) "But ye shall receive power, after that the Holy Ghost is come upon you: and ye shall be witnesses unto me both in Jerusalem, and in all Judaea, and in Samaria, and unto the uttermost part of the earth."

TUESDAY- MI DAILY DEVOTION
(Job 23: 14; Exodus 17:1-7)

"PROVISION"

"FOR HE PERFORMETH THE THINGS THAT HE APPOINTED FOR ME:"

14- "For he performeth the thing that is appointed for me: and many such things are with him."

PROVISION- Moses was tried and tested in the wilderness with the children of Israel. He was provoked when the children of Israel were in need of water and they were in intense thirst. I understand that the natural reaction would be to complain and have a negative remark. When the Israelites were in want for water, they chided Moses. They made Moses really angry at them for their attitude towards their leader and towards God. If you will just think of it, out of approximately 2.5 million people and assuming that 10% of them are believers, but out of those 10%, *no* one did ever came to Moses for prayer time and *no* one did ever suggested if they could gather together and pray and plan and think positively and how they could resolved the problem without complaining to God and Moses. I believe we have churches, homes and individual who are like that. It's just so easy for them to complain to God, to their pastors and leaders and even to their parents for small things and provision without even asking God first or trusting God for such.

The Lord showed them His provision already when they were in need of food in the wilderness of Sin. The children of Israel were stiff necked that they even wanted to kill Moses and counted him as a murderer. (Exodus 17:3-4)

3- "And the people thirsted there for water; and the people murmured against Moses, and said, Wherefore is this that thou hast brought us up out of Egypt, to kill us and our children and our cattle with thirst? 4- And Moses cried unto the LORD, saying, What shall I do unto this people? they be almost ready to stone me." No wonder they accused him of taking them to the wilderness to kill them and they wanted to stone him as Moses mentioned it in his prayer to God in verse 4- "they be almost ready to stone me." By the way, there are churches that are similar to the mixed congregation in the wilderness during the time of Moses. They don't care if their pastor and his family will starve…, they don't care if they're hurting the pastor emotionally, financially and morally as long as they satisfies their fleshly desire and attitude.

As a family and as a body of Christ, we can always come together in peace and love to pray for our needs. I love these verses and I remember my pastor, Dr. Pio S. Tica reading these verses to us in our prayer meeting service just before we pray as a church. It's in (Jeremiah 32:27; 17) 27-"Behold, I am the LORD, the God of all flesh: is there any thing too hard for me? 17- Ah Lord GOD! behold, thou hast made the heaven and the earth by thy great power and stretched out arm, and there is nothing too hard for thee:"

WEDNESDAY- MI DAILY DEVOTION
(Job 23:14)

PROVISION AND GOD'S MIRACLE IN THE MAKING...

23- "For he performeth the thing that is appointed for me: and many such things are with him."

Remember in the Book of Genesis at the time God was talking to Sarah about having a son? (Genesis 18:10- 14) 10- "Is any thing too hard for the LORD? At the time appointed I will return unto thee, according to the time of life, and Sarah shall have a son. 11- Then Sarah denied, saying, I laughed not; for she was afraid. And he said, Nay; but thou didst laugh. 12- Therefore Sarah laughed within herself, saying, After I am waxed old shall I have pleasure, my lord being old also? 13- And the LORD said unto Abraham, Wherefore did Sarah laugh, saying, Shall I of a surety bear a child, which am old? 14- Is any thing too hard for the LORD? At the time appointed I will return unto thee, according to the time of life, and Sarah shall have a son."

I believe that there's really nothing too hard for the Lord; but it's just too hard for us to pray and trust the Lord. The easy way out is to complain. And the easiest way for us Christians to do is to just LET GO of your desire, of your plans and dreams and for churches may be just to LET GO of that small or big projects, because of that great needs or financial difficulties. Our churches and our homes need the "3 H's". We need to put our HEARTS, our HEADS and our HANDS together for the Glory of our KING. You put your HEART together as you come to the throne of grace to pray and you put your heart together towards that project or vision. You put your heart together not for yourself, but for the Lord, for the edification of the body of Christ and for the lost. Any differences should be placed on the table of love and cooperation and unselfishly pray and consider it in the spirit of unity. I'm so proud of my church, the Philippine International Christian Church of Trenton, Michigan. If they don't agree with any agenda that we have in our meetings, they would just go over it or leave it on the table. Let me say this to some, just sleep over it. What happened during the time of Moses when the people were in need of water? Oh everyone wants to be a member of the resolution committee and their job descriptions were to complain, chide and have a negative attitude and have a wrong perspective. I hope you already see the picture? Put your HEART together because God's provision is on the way. After all the preparations... everything pays off as according to Apostle Paul. Notice Paul's testimony of God's provision as God uses the believers during his time to support him and the ministry God has entrusted to him.

Keep this in your heart when you're worried or in needs. (Philippians 4:16-19) 16- "For even in Thessalonica ye sent once and again unto my necessity. 17- Not because I desire a gift: but I desire fruit that may abound to your account. 18- But I have all, and abound: I am full, having received of Epaphroditus the things which were sent from you, an odour of a sweet smell, a sacrifice acceptable, wellpleasing to God. 19- But my God shall supply all your need according to his riches in glory by Christ Jesus."

THURSDAY- MI DAILY DEVOTION
(Matthew 6:33)

THEY PUT THEIR HEARTS TOGETHER

"But seek ye first the kingdom of God, and his righteousness; and all these things shall be added unto you."

Remember Abraham and Isaac's experienced when they put their HEART together for God and God alone. Their desires were God centered and they honored the Lord by their devotion, obedience and worship. And because of that, the Lord honored their faithfulness to His cause and the Lord's provision followed. I was thinking, may be Abraham has (Matthew 6:33) in his mind while he was obeying, walking and travelling on their way to the mountain in which it was only revealed to them later. We know it was Mount Moriah where they worship God and made the sacrifice; but they went anyways, not knowing where to go and sacrifice during those times, because they put God first in their life. Notice what Jesus said in (Matthew 6:33) "But seek ye first the kingdom of God, and his righteousness; and all these things shall be added unto you." Of course Abraham did not have the New Testament at the time, but he has the essence and element of the New Testament or (Matthew 6:33). We know and we believe that God does not change and has not changed and the principles of the Old Testament will not make any difference with the principles of the New Testament. The God of the Old Testament is the God of the New Testament and He is the same God that we worship and served. Abraham and Isaac's reaction to God's proposition was an act of faith. Obeying and putting Matthew 6:33 into practice and making it your life's principles is an act of faith. I believe this was missing in the lives of the children of Israel. Abraham acted in faith and step out of faith and Isaac followed. Moses took the step of faith and the children of Israel did not follow, but complained. Israel's attitude during those times was so opposite from Isaac's attitude when it comes to God. Compare Genesis 22 (the whole chapter) to Exodus 17 (the whole chapter) and you can see the difference between this group of people as opposite to Isaac and Abraham's character and attitude toward God. The issue of the lack of water sparks the bad conflict and confrontation between God's servants and God's people which also leads to the loss of confidence to its leadership. Notice here their journey as *according to the commandment of the Lord.* They were blessed as they were led by the pillar of cloud and fire, but it did not spare them from problems and one of the problems was water. We may be doing our duties and responsibilities for God, but it does not give us any guarantee that we will not meet any trouble or troubles in which God in His providence brings us into the trial of our faith and by His grace will keep us through.

Just imagine if the Apostle Paul was there during those times, I believe Paul would say the same thing to them based on (II Corinthians 5:7; 12: 9-10). 7- "(For we walk by faith, not by sight:) 9- And he said unto me, My grace is sufficient for thee: for my strength is made perfect in weakness. Most gladly therefore will I rather glory in my infirmities, that the power of Christ may rest upon me. 10- Therefore I take pleasure in infirmities, in reproaches, in necessities, in persecutions, in distresses for Christ's sake: for when I am weak, then am I strong."

FRIDAY MI DAILY DEVOTION
(Daniel 3: 3; 7)

THE ANCIENT WAR IN IRAQ

3- "Then the princes, the governors, and captains, the judges, the treasurers, the counsellors, the sheriffs, and all the rulers of the provinces, were gathered together unto the dedication of the image that Nebuchadnezzar the king had set up; and they stood before the image that Nebuchadnezzar had set up. 7- Therefore at that time, when all the people heard the sound of the cornet, flute, harp, sackbut, psaltery, and all kinds of music, all the people, the nations, and the languages, fell down and worshipped the golden image that Nebuchadnezzar the king had set up."

Babel was first mention in (Genesis 11: 9) "Therefore is the name of it called Babel; because the LORD did there confound the language of all the earth: and from thence did the LORD scatter them abroad upon the face of all the earth." *Babylon* means *confusion*. It was in this place where men tried to reach heaven by their own means. The Babylonians tried to make and start their own man- made religion. Iraq is the ancient Babylon. It was in ancient Babylon where God showed men that *He is the ruling God. He rules in the heart of men* and *He rules in the kingdom of men.* God is in control of everything. He just allows men to use their human power and wisdom to rule a country or a kingdom. (I Chronicles 29: 11) "Thine, O LORD, is the greatness, and the power, and the glory, and the victory, and the majesty: for all that is in the heaven and in the earth is thine; thine is the kingdom, O LORD, and thou art exalted as head above all." (Psalm 31:5) and (Luke 1: 68) "Blessed be the Lord God of Israel; for he hath visited and redeemed his people," (Galatians 3: 13) "Christ hath redeemed us from the curse of the law, being made a curse for us: for it is written, Cursed is every one that hangeth on a tree:" *He is the God who redeem* and He redeemed us from death and sin. God redeemed us from the punishment of hell and from hopelessness. God also redeemed us from the wrath of God. He redeemed us from the hand of our own king which is selfishness and greed. He is the God who is able to restore us. God is able to restore the broken relationship that we have. He is the only one who can restore any marred or broken relationships. It could be with your spouse, children, parents, friends, church or pastor. God is also able to restore the backslidden soldier of God. Anyone who had drifted from the faith can be restored by His grace and by the Blood of the Lamb. (Nehemiah 5: 11) "Restore, I pray you, to them, even this day, their lands, their vineyards, their olive yards, and their houses, also the hundredth part of the money, and of the corn, the wine, and the oil, that ye exact of them." *God is able to restore* our strength from weakness and being powerless. Check out the testimony of Shadrach, Meshach and Abednego: (Daniel 3:17) "If it be so, our God whom we serve is able to deliver us from the burning fiery furnace, and he will deliver us out of thine hand, O king." (Psalm 95:3- 6) "For the LORD is a great God, and a great King above all gods. 4- In his hand are the deep places of the earth: the strength of the hills is his also. 5- The sea is his, and he made it: and his hands formed the dry land. 6- O come, let us worship and bow down: let us kneel before the LORD our maker."

SATURDAY- MI DAILY DEVOTION
(Luke 17:5-10)

FAITH THAT WORKS…

5- "And the apostles said unto the Lord, Increase our faith. 6- And the Lord said, If ye had faith as a grain of mustard seed, ye might say unto this sycamine tree, Be thou plucked up by the root, and be thou planted in the sea; and it should obey you. 7- But which of you, having a servant plowing or feeding cattle, will say unto him by and by, when he is come from the field, Go and sit down to meat? 8- And will not rather say unto him, Make ready wherewith I may sup, and gird thyself, and serve me, till I have eaten and drunken; and afterward thou shalt eat and drink? 9- Doth he thank that servant because he did the things that were commanded him? I trow not. 10- So likewise ye, when ye shall have done all those things which are commanded you, say, We are unprofitable servants: we have done that which was our duty to do."

HANDS- While we were driving home from my appointment, I was talking to EJ my youngest son about him doing some homework, so he could help us with the responsibilities and chores in the house. And just like a regular kid, EJ made some excuses. Then, I started reciting to him a poem that I made randomly…

> *"It's good to play and watch and pray,*
> *But we need to toil our hand to soiled,*
>
> *We love to see what future holds; while*
> *working here our life unfold"*

And EJ said: "What's that…? You're weird dad, and I don't know what you're saying…", but I hope you like it. I may have sound weird to EJ, but there's truth to what I said to him.

There's absolutely nothing wrong with playing. And I'm positively and religiously with all my spiritual desire for watching and praying, but we also need to work together for the Kingdom. We should not only have to put our HEARTS together, but we also need to put our HANDS together. I'm for unity and for the possibilities. I like this principle: "I don't care who gets the credit as long as God gets the glory."

The only way we can lift the big boulder is for us to put our hands together. In the Philippines, there's a word that many Filipinos don't used anymore and that word is BAYANIHAN. Bayanihan means cooperative work without pay according to Felicidad T. E. Sagalongos. (Diksyunaryong Ingles- Filipino, Filipino- Ingles). We were called to do that for the Kingdom of God. And whenever we do the work of God and get to accomplished something for God and in the ministry, we gladly offer to God the honor and the glory. (Luke 17:10) "So likewise ye, when ye shall have done all those things which are commanded you, say, We are unprofitable servants: we have done that which was our duty to do." (Revelation 2:2-3) "I know thy works, and thy labour, and thy patience, and how thou canst not bear them which are evil: and thou hast tried them which say they are apostles, and are not, and hast found them liars: 3- And hast borne, and hast patience, and for my name's sake hast laboured, and hast not fainted."

SUNDAY- MI DAILY DEVOTION
(I Chronicles 16:27-31)

DO YOU TRUST THE PRESENCE OF GOD?

27- "Glory and honour are in his presence; strength and gladness are in his place. 28- Give unto the LORD, ye kindreds of the people, give unto the LORD glory and strength. 29- Give unto the LORD the glory due unto his name: bring an offering, and come before him: worship the LORD in the beauty of holiness. 30- Fear before him, all the earth: the world also shall be stable, that it be not moved. 31- Let the heavens be glad, and let the earth rejoice: and let men say among the nations, The LORD reigneth."

The previous verses talks about the Ark of God which symbolizes the presence of God. (I Chronicles 16:1) "So they brought the ark of God, and set it in the midst of the tent that David had pitched for it: and they offered burnt sacrifices and peace offerings before God."

The good thing about the church generation or grace period is that, we don't need the Ark of God, we don't need to have the Holy of holies and the animal sacrifices to be accepted and forgiven and feel His presence- the presence of God. Have you ever been to a church or chapel in which you can't even feel the presence of God? Have you ever been to a huge and beautiful churches and not even feel the presence of God? You felt like the worship service is just like a Senate session, some kind of a court session or a meeting and the only difference were the singing and offering. I've been to small churches and as you enter the door, you can already feel the spiritual struggle and it also happens even in big churches. What's wrong with those churches? How about individuals? Have you ever encountered someone who is a Christian and the first time you met that man or woman was… there's something in her or him. You can already feel the presence of God in that person as you have had your conversation with that Christian. I believe that that is one of the problems of many churches. They just go and get into the motion or flow. In every worship service or prayer meeting, they're just there and not even feel the presence of God and the worst thing that can happen is- they don't recognize God's presence already. Christians may get used to it, not feeling His presence in their private and public worship. That's one of the things that I would always ask God especially on Sundays before our worship starts. My prayer would be: "God make us feel your presence in our worship and in our midst…"

Not just in worship but in our daily walk with God, we should desire His presence and be conscious about it. In (Exodus 33:14-15) "And he said, My presence shall go with thee, and I will give thee rest. 15- And he said unto him, If thy presence go not with me, carry us not up hence." (II Chronicles 20:9) "If, when evil cometh upon us, as the sword, judgment, or pestilence, or famine, we stand before this house, and in thy presence, (for thy name is in this house,) and cry unto thee in our affliction, then thou wilt hear and help." (Psalm 140:13) "Surely the righteous shall give thanks unto thy name: the upright shall dwell in thy presence."

MONDAY- MI DAILY DEVOTION
(Exodus 33: 14- 16)

"MY PRESENCE SHALL GO WITH THEE..."

14- "And he said, My presence shall go with thee, and I will give thee rest. 15- And he said unto him, If thy presence go not with me, carry us not up hence. 16- For wherein shall it be known here that I and thy people have found grace in thy sight? is it not in that thou goest with us? so shall we be separated, I and thy people, from all the people that are upon the face of the earth."

Moses asked the Lord for the assurance of His presence with Israel as they marched to Canaan. Moses was not provocative to God as he asked Him to be with them. The children of Israel lost their favor from the Lord, because of their rebellion. They displeased the Lord, but Moses was always willing to stand for them and intercede to God in behalf of the children of Israel. Moses was the picture of the Lord Jesus Christ as he stood up to mediate to God in behalf of man. Sinners obtained grace, mercy and forgiveness through the intercessory work of Christ. According to Matthew Henry, "Thus, by the intercession of Christ, we obtain not only the removal of the curse, but an assurance of the blessing; we are not only saved from ruin, but become entitled to everlasting happiness." In verse number 12, Moses was so honest with God when he said: "See, thou sayest unto me, Bring up this people: and thou hast not let me know whom thou wilt send with me. Yet thou hast said, I know thee by name, and thou hast also found grace in my sight." "Lord, it is thou thyself that employest me; and wilt thou not own me? I am in the way of my duty; and shall I not have thy presence with me in that way?" Christians and churches must desire and long for God's presence in worship and God's way in their walk with God. As you worship God and desire to do your Christian service, I hope and pray that we would be like Moses who prayed for God's presence and direction. Moses also desires to know Him more and that he would find grace in His (God's) sight. (Exodus 33:13) In spite of the bad economy that the United States of America is going through right now, it is still better off compared to many other countries in the world. And the sad thing about those who live with so much in this world is that, they don't really care about God's presence in their lives. They're just so busy with their thing or things, that they don't pay so much attention to God's presence in their life. Moses said, if I really found grace in your sight, then show me your way. If I will put it in my own words, it would be- "If I have found grace in your sight, then show me the map, show me the floor plan and your will for me and your people, tell me exactly what you want, where to go and what to do… And make it really clear and plain to me…" But God's answer was clear in verse 14- "And he said, My presence shall go with thee, and I will give thee rest." His presence is our assurance.

The only reason why you don't want God's presence and want to run away from the presence of God is, if you were in the same situation of Adam and Eve after the fall of man or you're in Jonah's situations. (Genesis 3:8) "And they heard the voice of the LORD God walking in the garden in the cool of the day: and Adam and his wife hid themselves from the presence of the LORD God amongst the trees of the garden."

TUESDAY- MI DAILY DEVOTION
(Galatians 6:9-10)

"GIVE 'EM THE THUMB'S UP!

9- "And let us not be weary in well doing: for in due season we shall reap, if we faint not. 10- As we have therefore opportunity, let us do good unto all men, especially unto them who are of the household of faith."

We often fail to recognized or give people, an employee, a pastor or fellow believers a tap in their back for doing a "Job well done". And even in a very little things and not so significant accomplishment deserves an appreciation, especially those things that were done in the Name of Christ. Parents and churches should learn to give proper esteem to those who works and really worked hard for its cause. Christians should learn to follow the example of Apostle Paul. Paul gave his followers a *THUMB'S UP* as they served the Lord in their area of responsibilities and ministry. A sentence or a word of commendation or may be just a simple show of your appreciation can change an individual's life. And you can make an impact by just giving them a tap in their back. Check out Paul's THUMB'S UP to a brother in the Lord like Epaphras. (Colossians 1:7-8). If the "Plaque of Appreciation" was available during Paul's time, Paul could have given him one for being a faithful servant of the Lord. Paul was also talking about him (Epaphras) as his fellow prisoner and fellow laborer. (Philemon 1:23; 24). It's so easy to be proud of someone who has a good position in the government or of a big company, but it will be a different story to others to be proud of someone who is a laborer and a prisoner of Christ. (Colossians 4:12-13) I know that the name "Epaphras" is not a very popular name to many of you, but I believe in heaven, it is. And if Epaphras will be speaking in your church and your pastor will introduce him to the congregation, this would be how your pastor may give the introduction for Mr. Epaphras: "Today, we are so privileged to have with us as our speaker for this very special day and event in this great church of the Lord. We have with us a special person to grace this special occasion. It's a great privilege for me to stand with this great man of God and introduce to you the fellow servant of Apostle Paul. Mr. Epaphras is a faithful minister of Christ and a prayer warrior. He was responsible in spreading the word to the believers about your love in the Spirit. He was Paul's fellow prisoner and laborer in Christ Jesus. Please welcome the gentleman who suffered with Apostle Paul in prison. The prisoner for the sake of the gospel and of the Lord… Epaphras!!! If you are a "Title Conscious" or let me say "Title Centered" individual, Epaphras' resume is not very impressive. No doctorate degree, not even a high school diploma, but his life, his experienced and his love for the Lord speaks louder than any great position or title in life. And Paul commended Epaphras for such love and dedication for the Lord and His works. Imagine if Epaphras is with us today and you will quote these verses to him, I believe you will hear a loud AMEN…!!! (I Corinthians 15:57-58) 57- "But thanks be to God, which giveth us the victory through our Lord Jesus Christ.58- Therefore, my beloved brethren, be ye stedfast, unmoveable, always abounding in the work of the Lord, forasmuch as ye know that your labour is not in vain in the Lord."

WEDNESDAY- MI DAILY DEVOTION
(Philippians 2:25)

"EPAPHRODITUS…!!!? WHO NAMED YOU*%^@!&!#?"

25- "Yet I supposed it necessary to send to you Epaphroditus, my brother, and companion in labour, and fellowsoldier, but your messenger, and he that ministered to my wants."

Do you like your name? I like my name, but when I was a little boy; I hated my name, because I felt like I was the only "Ely" in the world except for an actor of the Tarzan movie named Ron Ely which was actually a last name. And when I became a teenager, I realized, I really have a unique and Bible name. How about Mait (Mah-it) or Boklit (Book-lit) or Potot (Pooootoot) or may be Maak (Mah-act) Nene Amo (Neeh-nee Ahm-moo). They all don't sounds so good to you. They're weird names, no actually nicknames. But they are real people. People with emotions, love and they are people with souls and spirit like other people with beautiful names and nicknames. They are just like those people who are better off financially and materially. One day I was at the store and the sales lady was reading my name on my driver's license and debit card and said, "I have a grandson with this same name, not many people has this name…" And you will not name your son Epaphroditus, it doesn't really sound that good. "Epaphroditus" means "Charming"; He was Paul's best friend, a gentile believer who ministered to Paul in behalf of his church. (Philippians 2:25) "Yet I supposed it necessary to send to you Epaphroditus, my brother, and companion in labour, and fellowsoldier, but your messenger, and he that ministered to my wants." Epaphroditus was one of the best examples of a responsible and faithful Christian.

He lived a life that was fully surrendered to God, His cause and ministry. Notice of how he spent his life and time for the Lord: he served the Lord, the Apostle Paul and the church- out of love. Paul and Epaphroditus serves the same God and Father as recorded in verse 25 when Paul called him "brother." They were serving the Lord not for personal benefit and interests, but out of love- love for God and people. He also served the Lord and labour for God with sincerity of heart. (Verse 25) "...Epaphroditus, my brother, and companion in labour," It was Paul who gave him the positive remarks about his heart and service for his people and church. (Amos 8:7) "The LORD hath sworn by the excellency of Jacob, Surely I will never forget any of their works." (Revelation 3:8) "I know thy works: behold, I have set before thee an open door, and no man can shut it: for thou hast a little strength, and hast kept my word..." Apostle Paul called him "fellow soldier." It means they wear the same uniform, in the same cause, with the same discipline, bound for the same danger, serving the same Master and General, going through the same struggle, in the same duty. As soldiers, they were bound to follow orders from their Superior. Paul and Epaphroditus were serving the same LORD. And Epaphroditus supported Paul in prison. (II Timothy 2:2-5) 2- "Thou therefore, my son, be Strong in the grace that is in Christ Jesus. 3- Thou therefore endure hardness, as a good soldier of Jesus Christ. 4- No man that warreth entangleth himself with the affairs of this life; that he may please him who hath chosen him to be a soldier. 5- And if a man also strive for masteries, yet is he not crowned, except he strive lawfully."

THURSDAY- MI DAILY DEVOTION
(Philippians 2:25-30)

EPAPHRODITUS... IS TERMINAL?

25- "Yet I supposed it necessary to send to you Epaphroditus, my brother, and companion in labour, and fellowsoldier, but your messenger, and he that ministered to my wants.- 26- For he longed after you all, and was full of heaviness, because that ye had heard that he had been sick. 27- For indeed he was sick nigh unto death: but God had mercy on him; and not on him only, but on me also, lest I should have sorrow upon sorrow. 28- I sent him therefore the more carefully, that, when ye see him again, ye may rejoice, and that I may be the less sorrowful. 29- Receive him therefore in the Lord with all gladness; and hold such in reputation: 30- Because for the work of Christ he was nigh unto death, not regarding his life, to supply your lack of service toward me."

Have you ever heard of a friend, a sibling or a brother in the Lord who faithfully served God and is living a holy life and really loves the Lord and family; and then... there comes the news... that individual is sick or that individual has a cancer and was given few months to live. Picture in your mind the devastation it could bring in the family and friends. The family and people that surrounded him or her may start questioning God. It happened to Paul and Epaphroditus. (Philippians 2:26) Epaphras and Epaphroditus did not have any dialogue in the Bible. Actions speak louder than words, as they say. If this was a movie, their role was seems insignificant to the movie, but they were the ones who really made the difference. Paul was the one who talked to them and speak for them and this was the moment where Paul may have problems spreading the news- the bad news about Epaphroditus' terminal sickness. That would be one of the hardest thing to comprehend when bad things happens to good people. And also, it would be hard to explain with this kind of situation to a growing Christians or new believers. (Philippians 2:27) "For indeed he was sick nigh unto death: but God had mercy on him; and not on him only, but on me also, lest I should have sorrow upon sorrow." "Epaphroditus was nigh unto death." Many of us Christians could not really identify with Epaphroditus' situation being "nigh unto death…" Here's a soldier of the Lord Jesus Christ who was willing to live for Christ and also ready to die in the name of the Lord Jesus Christ and willing to die for the cause of Christ. (Philippians 2:30) I like that phrase; "… not regarding his life…" It must be hard for Paul to tell everybody about Epaphroditus sickness unto death, but it was harder for Epaphroditus to understand his situation. He could question God like: "In spite of my love and faithfulness Lord, you let this sickness come my way…? Who will take over my ministry and who will take care and support my family? And of course we're here to love and to be faithful in the Lord. Just like a wedding vow: "For richer, for poorer, for better and for worse; in sickness and in health, to have and to hold. From this day forward, cleaving to you alone, 'till death or the rapture of the church comes, I am yours and I will love you and serve you" What Paul was saying to young Timothy, he was also saying this to Epaphroditus and to all of us. "But I trust in the Lord…" (Philippians 2:20-21; 24) 20- "For I have no man likeminded, who will naturally care for your state. 21- For all seek their own, not the things which are Jesus Christ's."

FRIDAY- MI DAILY DEVOTION
(Philippians 2:30)

EPAPHRODITUS... DID YOU HAVE A BALANCED DIET OR A BALANCED LIFE?

30- "Because for the work of Christ he was nigh unto death, not regarding his life, to supply your lack of service toward me."

People have the tendency to seek their own glory and get some credit to some success or accomplishment even in the expense of others. (Proverbs 27:2) "Let another man praise thee..." Some may even step on someone else's ladder to get what they want and to make it to the top echelon. But not with Paul who gives "tribute to whom tribute is due." (Romans 13:6-7) 6- "For for this cause pay ye tribute also: for they are God's ministers, attending continually upon this very thing. 7- Render therefore to all their dues: tribute to whom tribute is due; custom to whom custom; fear to whom fear; honour to whom honour." Apostle Paul put the verses into practice in the lives of Epaphras and Epaphroditus when Paul gave them the commendation. If I was in Epaphroditus' shoes, it would really be easier to get motivated and to live a balanced life... No wonder, this unsung hero and great man of God was a blessing and a testimony of God's grace even in near death. Epaphroditus tried to live a balanced life. Epaphroditus' sickness was beyond his control. Others got sick because they abused their body and systems. Sometimes sickness can just come without any warnings. We must have a good and proper diet and religiously watch our diet and really be disciplined in our intake. And we need to get some physical exercises for us to be physically fit. At the same time, we also need to be mentally fit. It means we need to be sharp in our thinking process and be a Christian who is full of wisdom and knowledge. We need to read all kinds of good books and really read our Bible daily. Christians should also be strong in their spiritual life, so we would not be overcome and destroyed by our enemy- the devil. Balanced is important in Christian life and Epaphroditus was a balanced Christian. It's good to love the Word of God and to witness to others about Jesus, but don't forget to work and work hard for the Lord and in the ministry. It's good to always walk by faith, but we also need to worship Him on Sundays. It's good to be in the fellowship, but we also need to exercise our faith daily. I heard a story in the Philippines about a church that has monthly theme and caption that they would usually put up on the stage. On one occasion the church theme was "JESUS ONLY…" Some of the captions were only made of carton or paper and most of the church windows are open. One day the wind blows off J-E-S from the caption which it left them the words "…US ONLY." As you may have observed it in some organizations or churches which I believe is really not a good practice. Some churches or groups, they have that principles or attitude in life: "just US and US only." They are the group of people who are not a balanced Christians. You can set aside your differences and your legalistic views and just have one focus. Not with Paul, Epaphroditus and the Philippian church. They work as a team and Paul was the team leader and they have the same focus- *Christ and for His Glory*. (Colossians 3: 1-2) 1- "If ye then be risen with Christ, seek those things which are above, where Christ sitteth on the right hand of God. 2- Set your affection on things above, not on things on the earth."

SATURDAY- MI DAILY DEVOTION
(Philippians 2:25-30)

EPAPHRODITUS – COULD YOU TAKE A BREAK?

25- "Yet I supposed it necessary to send to you Epaphroditus, my brother, and companion in labour, and fellowsoldier, but your messenger, and he that ministered to my wants. 26- For he longed after you all, and was full of heaviness, because that ye had heard that he had been sick. 27- For indeed he was sick nigh unto death: but God had mercy on him; and not on him only, but on me also, lest I should have sorrow upon sorrow. 28- I sent him therefore the more carefully, that, when ye see him again, ye may rejoice, and that I may be the less sorrowful. 29- Receive him therefore in the Lord with all gladness; and hold such in reputation: 30- Because for the work of Christ he was nigh unto death, not regarding his life, to supply your lack of service toward me."

Yes sir, could you take a break… please, just for a moment or a day? That was the suggestion of the secretary to her boss in their conversation to her boss' office. And that's very true, I believe that that could be a good question to the politicians, pastors, parents, doctors and people who can't spell, say and write the words "break", "slow down", "sit and be still", "quite time" and other words that pertains to just be alone and be quiet with God. While I'm writing this portion of MI DAILY DEVOTION, I'm in my hotel room with my wife. The ladies from my church are having a ladies outing and they decided to spend it in a hotel and have some swimming time and beauty moment. And I went with them and got a room with my wife and spent alone in my hotel room, because I wanted to be alone and undisturbed. No phone calls, no television, no one would ask you questions and ask for something. I suggested to my wife if we could do this, staying in a hotel room at least twice or once a month for us to get away and be alone with God and read.

Notice the advice and reminder of the writer of the Book of Psalm, (Psalms 46:11) "Be still, and know that I am God: I will be exalted among the heathen, I will be exalted in the earth." Even the Lord Jesus Christ went to the desert place just to be alone. (Mark 6:31-32) "And he said unto them, Come ye yourselves apart into a desert place, and rest a while: for there were many coming and going, and they had no leisure so much as to eat. 32- And they departed into a desert place by ship privately." If Christ, the Son of God have the time to rest and be in the desert place to be away from the multitudes, I believe we can do the same. It's good to be ON THE GO, but we also need to take a break. We sometimes would just let the machines and engines rest for a while so it won't overheat and break. Burned out is the enemy that hits many pastors and Christians as well. God may have let Epaphroditus lay on his bed sick, so the Lord could minister to him. The Christians whom he ministered unto could have done the same. Check out what Isaiah said in (Isaiah 41:1) "Keep silence before me, O islands; and let the people renew their strength: let them come near; then let them speak: let us come near together to judgment." (Isaiah 40:31) "But they that wait upon the LORD shall renew their strength; they shall mount up with wings as eagles; they shall run, and not be weary; and they shall walk, and not faint."

SUNDAY- MI DAILY DEVOTION
(Luke 22: 31- 62)

THE DOWNFALL OF PETER

Peter's life as a Christian was full of failures and blunders. Peter's downfall was not sudden but gradual. Peter's life is very much like ours. (I Corinthians 10: 12) "Wherefore let him that thinketh he standeth take heed lest he fall." (Proverbs 14: 14) "The backslider in heart shall be filled with his own ways: and a good man shall be satisfied from himself."

PETER'S SELF CONFIDENCE (Luke 22:33) "And he said unto him, Lord, I am ready to go with thee, both in prison, and to death." He trusted himself and his ability as well as his own strength instead of God. Although the Lord warned Peter of the coming temptation, yet Peter just took it for granted or he might have just took the Lord's Word so lightly. Peter trusted in himself and in the flesh. Peter might have thought he would remain faithful to God. (Luke 22: 31-32).

PETER GAVE UP HIS PRAYER LIFE (Luke 22: 45- 46) 45 "And when he arose up from prayer, and was come to his disciples, he found them sleeping for sorrow, 46- And said unto them, Why sleep ye? rise and pray, lest ye enter into temptation."

(Matthew 26: 40- 41) 40- "And he cometh unto the disciples, and findeth them asleep, and saith unto Peter, What, could ye not watch with me one hour? 41- Watch and pray, that ye enter not into temptation; the spirit indeed is willing, but the flesh is weak."

This was Peter's second downward step to his downfall. He did not learn to call to God for help which was really the primary cause of his backsliding. It was really prayerlessness. How many times have we felt like praying, but your body and mind seem so tired to pray. Your spirit is willing to pray but your flesh is not. Your spirit said, talk to God but your flesh, your body is saying the different thing, it's saying the opposite. Your body is saying, "You go to bed and sleep", The Holy Spirit of God said, "You must go to church". "You read your Bible." but your flesh says, "NO".

PETER BECAME CARNAL AND WORLDLY (Luke 22:49-50) 49- "When they which were about him saw what would follow, they said unto him, Lord, shall we smite with the sword? 50- "And one of them smote the servant of the high priest, and cut off his right ear." Peter was acting in the flesh. He cut off the ear of Malchus. Peter "walked" "standing up" "sits" with those who do not know, with those who do not love the Lord and with those who do not honour the Lord; "Worldliness is anything, and everything in which the Lord is left out." Peter was brave and loyal to our Lord, but he was not acting as spiritual and as a mature Christian.

A good reminder for us Christians in spiritual sense; don't walk, stand and sit with sinners… and you'll be blessed by the Lord. (Psalms 1:1) "BLESSED is the man that walketh not in the counsel of the ungodly, nor standeth in the way of sinners, nor sitteth in the seat of the scornful."

MONDAY- MI DAILY DEVOTION
(Isaiah 45: 22)

"LOOK UNTO ME, AND BE SAVED…"

22- "Look unto me, and be ye saved, all the ends of the earth: for I am God, and there is none else"

A year ago, I was in London, England. I had the privileged to visit the church of Charles Haddon Spurgeon. He was the prince of preachers during his time. The chapel was so beautiful and I noticed that the caption up in the stage was the same as what I have heard. I heard that the caption has never been changed or replaced since the time of Charles H. Spurgeon which says: "Look unto me, and be ye saved." The Lord has the same message to every generation: And it has not changed… "Look unto Him (God) by faith and be saved."

(Isaiah 42: 18) "Hear, ye deaf; and look, ye blind, that ye may see." "Hear, ye deaf" No way!!! "… and look, ye blind," Impossible!!! That could be the conclusions of the unbelieving world. Those are the words and the remarks that you will hear from the sarcastic in which you can't really pressed things like that in their ears. But, this is a great message for every man and woman in the world. You may not be deaf and blind physically, but you are deaf and blind spiritually if you don't have the Lord Jesus Christ in your heart. It shows us the importance and the need to listen to God's Word and our need to look up to God by faith and be saved. "Hear ye deaf…" "…and look, ye blind…" How can it be? How can those things be possible? Sounds like the same questions Mary asked when she was confronted by an angel about Jesus being born through her. (Luke 1:30- 35)

30-"And the angel said unto her, Fear not, Mary: for thou hast found favour with God. 31- And, behold, thou shalt conceive in thy womb, and bring forth a son, and shalt call his name JESUS. 32- He shall be great, and shall be called the Son of the Highest: and the Lord God shall give unto him the throne of his father David: 33- And he shall reign over the house of Jacob for ever; and of his kingdom there shall be no end. 34- Then said Mary unto the angel, How shall this be, seeing I know not a man? 35- And the angel answered and said unto her, The Holy Ghost shall come upon thee, and the power of the Highest shall overshadow thee: therefore also that holy thing which shall be born of thee shall be called the Son of God." If the question is: "How can this be? Then the straight answer would be: Verse 35 "And the angel answered and said unto her, The Holy Ghost shall come upon thee, and the power of the Highest shall overshadow thee:" If this verse applies to Mary, it applies to us too. Unless the Holy Spirit of God will come upon us and God would put His arms around us, so we could have His grace to receive His Word and the Lord Jesus Christ. We will never be enlightened by His Word and will never be saved apart from His grace. Another good answer to those questions would be in verse 37- "For with God nothing shall be impossible."

(Zechariah 12: 10) "And I will pour upon the house of David, and upon the inhabitants of Jerusalem, the spirit of grace and of supplications: and they shall look upon me whom they have pierced, and they shall mourn for him, as one mourneth for his only son, and shall be in bitterness for him, as one that is in bitterness for his firstborn." It's very clear that this verse was talking about the Lord Jesus Christ. The verse was a prophecy of the death of the Lord Jesus Christ. This was from the Old Testament, but the Scriptures were talking already about the future generations and about how the future generations could obtain salvation through Him whom they have pierced." (John 8:14) "Jesus answered and said unto them, Though I bear record of myself, yet my record is true: for I know whence I came, and whither I go; but ye cannot tell whence I come, and whither I go."(John 19:34-37).

TUESDAY- MI DAILY DEVOTION
(Philippians 2:25-30)

EPAPHRODITUS - BURDENED AND BLESSED!!!

25- "Yet I supposed it necessary to send to you Epaphroditus, my brother, and companion in labour, and fellowsoldier, but your messenger, and he that ministered to my wants. 26- For he longed after you all, and was full of heaviness, because that ye had heard that he had been sick. 27- For indeed he was sick nigh unto death: but God had mercy on him; and not on him only, but on me also, lest I should have sorrow upon sorrow. 28- I sent him therefore the more carefully, that, when ye see him again, ye may rejoice, and that I may be the less sorrowful. 29- Receive him therefore in the Lord with all gladness; and hold such in reputation: 30- Because for the work of Christ he was nigh unto death, not regarding his life, to supply your lack of service toward me."

Epaphroditus has the same burden like many of us. Sickness indeed is a very common problem at home and to individuals. Even ministers and good Christians are not spared from such. Apostle Paul has his own "thorn in the flesh, burdens and weaknesses. (II Corinthians 12:5-10). I was in a hospital several times last year 2009 and last January of 2010 due to some physical problems. Some of my friends who are close to me and have visited me in my hospital bed teased me of my being so frequent in a hospital. They said that I always spend my vacation time in the hospital. A pastor friend of mine said that I was investing in the hospital while others made a comment like, "so, you really want to maximize your insurance". Some of my pastor friends would jokingly tell me that I'm already one of the stockholders of the hospital.

But those days that I was in a hospital were one of my best days that I have in my life. God dealt with me in so many things and in so many ways and with my sin. He humbled me that I learned to really trust Him even in a smallest and seems insignificant things in my life. I believe that reading these verses from the Book of Matthew over and over is not a waste of our time. (Matthew 11:28-30) 28- "Come unto me, all ye that labour and are heavy laden, and I will give you rest. 29- Take my yoke upon you, and learn of me; for I am meek and lowly in heart: and ye shall find rest unto your souls. 30- For my yoke is easy, and my burden is light."

Sometimes when people are visiting you in your hospital bed, you can see from their eyes the love, the care, the pain and also the pity. Others are annoying and tried to make you feel guilty. Just like what Job said to his friends, they're miserable comforters. But I felt, I was better off than my visitors and anybody else in the world, because of what God was doing in my heart. That's the thing that people don't see. That was the thing that really made the difference with other people out there, whether they are in the most luxurious hotel or mansion. And they can be in a theater, in a great concert or park; but it's just an outward happiness, while mine was an inward joy in spite of the pain I was going through.

(Philippians 4:4) "Rejoice in the Lord alway: and again I say, Rejoice." (I Thessalonians 5:16-18) 16- "Rejoice evermore. 17- Pray without ceasing. 18- In every thing give thanks: for this is the will of God in Christ Jesus concerning you."

WEDNESDAY- MI DAILY DEVOTION
(Philippians 4:6-7; 19)

LOOK UP TO GOD FOR YOUR NEEDS

6- "Be careful for nothing; but in every thing by prayer and supplication with thanksgiving let your requests be made known unto God. 7- And the peace of God, which passeth all understanding, shall keep your hearts and minds through Christ Jesus." 19- "But my God shall supply all your need according to his riches in glory by Christ Jesus."

What else do you want and need from me? That was the question of the husband to his wife when they have an argument about money. "I gave you everything you need and want and you are still asking for more... what else do you want and need?" I believe that no matter what you have and what you possess, you will still be in need. You are in need of God's love, in need of understanding or in need of support and guidance, wisdom or knowledge. We are all a needy people. The billionaires, the millionaires and the bum or homeless are all needy people and we are all living with needs. We have different needs, but for sure we have needs. Your environment and economic or financial condition will not spare you from having needs.

In (Ephesians 6:18) "Praying always with all prayer and supplication in the Spirit, and watching thereunto with all perseverance and supplication for all saints;" Paul, by the guidance and leading of the Holy Spirit of God did not just write this verse for the prisoners, pastors and missionaries or the less fortunate, but for every person who came to know the Lord Jesus Christ; and even for those in authority. This was written even for the kings and for the wealthy. (Isaiah

45:14) "Thus saith the LORD, The labour of Egypt, and merchandise of Ethiopia and of the Sabeans, men of stature, shall come over unto thee, and they shall be thine: they shall come after thee; in chains they shall come over, and they shall fall down unto thee, they shall make supplication unto thee, saying, Surely God is in thee; and there is none else, there is no God." (Philippians 4:6) "Be careful for nothing; but in every thing by prayer and supplication with thanksgiving let your requests be made known unto God." There are 3 important things that Paul mentioned in this verse: 1- Prayer, 2- Supplication and 3- Thanksgiving. Therefore, as believers; we must practice and be serious about our prayer life and we must always be thankful to God in all things. God wants for us to pray and pray to God with thanksgiving.

(I Timothy 2:1) "I exhort therefore, that, first of all, supplications, prayers, intercessions, and giving of thanks, be made for all men;"

God knows the future and He has abundant supply to everyone who asks in faith and humility.

1- God wants for us to expect His answers and blessings.

2- God wants for us to experience His great blessings and share it to others in need.

3- God wants for us to enjoy it and be a channel of blessing with what God have for us, may it be spiritual, material or financial.

In (Genesis 12:1-3) 1-"Now the LORD had said unto Abram, Get thee out of thy country, and from thy kindred, and from thy father's house, unto a land that I will show thee: 2- And I will make of thee a great nation, and I will bless thee, and make thy name great; and thou shalt be a blessing: 3- And I will bless them that bless thee, and curse him that curseth thee: and in thee shall all families of the earth be blessed."

THURSDAY- MI DAILY DEVOTION
(Philippians 2:26-27)

A TESTIMONY OF GOD'S GRACE, (God's healing to Epaphroditus and to a brother in the Lord)

26- "For he longed after you all, and was full of heaviness, because that ye had heard that he had been sick. 27- For indeed he was sick nigh unto death: but God had mercy on him; and not on him only, but on me also, lest I should have sorrow upon sorrow."

Here's a great Testimony of Rev. Gary MacManamy. He is the team leader and director of evangelism of the Baptist State Convention of Michigan. I first heard of his testimony at our Language meeting and I was so blessed. I can relate to his testimony and I know exactly what he felt and experienced with God during those difficult and near death experienced. Just like what Epaphroditus went through, God's grace was sufficient for him and for brother Gary MacManamy. Here's his story...

"At the conclusion of the GPS Committee meeting at NAMB (North American Mission Board) last October 30; I boarded the flight to Detroit from Atlanta, Georgia. Upon cabin pressure changed at take off, the first of four heart attacked took place. None of the symptoms were remindful of a heart attack. Each lasted about 10 minutes. The first episode was at take off, the second at landing, then the third in my car and the fourth just about 30 minutes later, I was still in my car. Upon the fourth attacked, I reached into the glove compartment and took a handful of 81 mg aspirin and as it began to dawn on me. I knew that it was a heart problem. I headed straight to an urgent care location which transported me to a nearby hospital where two stints were put into two clogged arteries within my heart. Five days later, I went home. Two weeks later I went back to work. In my office while visiting with co-workers, I voiced something that I haven't been able to quit talking about since… simply this, "I wouldn't have missed that episode in my life for anything. If God took me back to just before that moment and asked me if I would want to miss it, what would I say? My answer would be that I would go through it again. Because I now know God better than I have ever known Him… I know His love better, His Almightiness better and His presence better. I wouldn't have missed it for anything. Not only that, but I know my wife and her love better, my family's love better, friend's love as well as co-workers love better and on and on it goes."

What I've learned is that God uses those kinds of moments for two things. First, He allows those moments to get one's attention. It would depend on the needs and as how God would draw us closer to Him more deeply. God wants to get our attention from things and it would also depend on the needs for conforming to God. Secondly, He allows those moments to draw a crowd that He would get the glory. Nobody acts more like God than God. I wouldn't have missed those difficult months for anything. What an incredible God."

(I Peter 2:24) "Who his own self bare our sins in his own body on the tree, that we, being dead to sins, should live unto righteousness: by whose stripes ye were healed."

FRIDAY- MI DAILY DEVOTION
(Romans 6: 19; 22)

SANCTIFICATION – WHERE IN THE WORLD THIS WORD CAME FROM…?

19- "I speak after the manner of men because of the infirmity of your flesh: for as ye have yielded your members servants to uncleanness and to iniquity unto iniquity; even so now yield your members servants to righteousness unto holiness." 22- "But now being made free from sin, and become servants to God, ye have your fruit unto holiness, and the end everlasting life."

The noun "sanctification" is found several times in the New Testament. If you are a believer of the Lord Jesus Christ, you very well know that great changed in you. You are aware of the difference that you have in your life as a Christian. There were changes in your life, in your perspective, in your ways and in your heart. (I Corinthians 1:30) "But of him are ye in Christ Jesus, who of God is made unto us wisdom, and righteousness, and sanctification, and redemption:" How do you like that package deal from God through the Lord Jesus Christ? The last two is good enough for me: sanctification and redemption. But the first one could be the greatest, because if you have the first one which is: "But of him are ye in Christ Jesus." You have everything if you have Christ in you, because Christ is the owner of all things, the Heaven of heavens and the earth and everything under the earth. (I Thessalonians 4:3-4) "For this is the will of God, even your sanctification, that ye should abstain from fornication: 4- That every one of you should know how to possess his vessel in sanctification and honour;" Some of the pastors and the congregations felt some discomfort, and very uneasy when you talk about sin, if it's about adultery and fornication. There are members of some of the congregations who are divorced or have an extra marital affair or have committed adultery. Someone told me about the problem of the couples in his congregation. And I asked him, what seems to be the problem? The pastor said: "Cheating is the name of the game…? Indeed, to others; it's just a game that they wanted to play, not knowing that they are hurting someone on the other side of the fence and they are destroying homes and the future of the kids. Some of the words that are akin to sanctification are:

Holiness (Romans 1: 4) "And declared to be the Son of God with power, according to the spirit of holiness, by the resurrection from the dead:" We need that kind of Spirit- the Spirit of holiness. We've watch so much of the bad spirits, evil spirits, spirit of greed and selfishness that we need to see some spirit of holiness. Be it at your church, on television or at work. We need that kind of spirit. We see it in the life of the Lord Jesus Christ and on some of Christ's disciples like the Apostle Paul and we need to see it in the life of the present day Christians. So, sanctification means holiness as Paul mentioned in (Romans 1:4). We have the spirit of holiness because of Him who is Holy.

Holy (Acts 7: 33) "Then said the Lord to him, Put off thy shoes from thy feet: for the place where thou standest is holy ground." I've been thinking about this for a long time. If 10 years before you die and God would ask you to spend 5 minutes of your time so you could be a better Christian and so you will have more passion for God and the lost world… where would you have it? Would you spend that 10 minutes at the feet of Jesus in Holy ground or in hell with Satan and his angels and with those who rejected the salvation offered to us by God? A classmate of mine from the Bible College said something about sanctification with broken English and accent… "… Sanctification means holy and holy means sanctification."

Saint (I Corinthians 16: 1) "Now concerning the collection for the saints, as I have given order to the churches of Galatia, even so do ye."

The saints are the sanctified and the sanctified are the saints. All believers are the saints of God and we are not the saints of an organization or religious group, but the saints of God. We were made Holy by the Blood of the Lamb that was slain for the salvation of men. (Revelation 12:11) "And they overcame him by the blood of the Lamb, and by the word of their testimony; and they loved not their lives unto the death." (Revelation 14:4) "These are they which were not defiled with women; for they are virgins. These are they which follow the Lamb whithersoever he goeth. These were redeemed from among men, being the firstfruits unto God and to the Lamb."

The Sanctuary (Hebrews 8: 2) "A minister of the sanctuary, and of the true tabernacle, which the Lord pitched, and not man." Remember the Holy of holies? We don't have the Holy of holies, because it was only in the Old Testament, but we have the throne of grace where we could come through our Lord Jesus Christ. He is our sanctuary and our Holy of holies.

Sanctify or hallow (Matthew 6: 9) "After this manner therefore pray ye: Our Father which art in heaven, Hallowed be thy name." (Exodus 19:14) "And Moses went down from the mount unto the people, and sanctified the people; and they washed their clothes. (II Chronicles 29:17) "Now they began on the first day of the first month to sanctify, and on the eighth day of the month came they to the porch of the LORD: so they sanctified the house of the LORD in eight days; and in the sixteenth day of the first month they made an end."

SATURDAY- MI DAILY DEVOTION
(Revelation 2: 19)

THE CHRISTIAN WORKER...

19- "I know thy works, and charity, and service, and faith, and thy patience, and thy works; and the last to be more than the first."

A- ACTIVATE YOUR FAITH (Hebrews 11: 1- 3; 6) 1- "Now faith is the substance of things hoped for, the evidence of things not seen. 2- For by it the elders obtained a good report. 3- Through faith we understand that the worlds were framed by the word of God, so that things which are seen were not made of things which do appear. 6- But without faith it is impossible to please him: for he that cometh to God must believe that he is, and that he is a rewarder of them that diligently seek him." You already have that faith when you accept Jesus in your heart. Our faith in God must be active and a working faith not a dead faith.

B- BE SINCERE WITH WHAT YOU DO FOR THE LORD. (Philippians 1: 10) "That ye may approve things that are excellent; that ye may be sincere and without offence till the day of Christ;" Sincerity for Paul is not a 1 time thing or temporary attitude towards God. For Apostle Paul, sincerity is for life. It is until the day of the Lord Jesus Christ. (Joshua 24: 14) "Now therefore fear the LORD, and serve him in sincerity and in truth: and put away the gods which your fathers served on the other side of the flood, and in Egypt; and serve ye the LORD."

C- COMMIT EVERYTHING TO GOD. When you commit everything to God, it would mean that we don't have any hand on anything that you have laid on the feet of Jesus. When you offer your life, your talents, your burdens, your giving to God and whatever you may lay down in the feet of Jesus; they're not yours, they're in the hands of God already… everything belongs to God. (I Peter 5: 7) "Casting all your care upon him; for he careth for you."

D- DEVELOP YOUR GIFTS. It's not about what you know and how much you know and how talented and gifted you are… it's about your willingness to give up and be used of God. It's about how willing you are to God as you let Him use you and how willing you are to give your talents and gifts to God and for His glory. (I Corinthians 12: 31; 14: 12) 31- "But covet earnestly the best gifts: and yet show I unto you a more excellent way." 12- Even so ye, forasmuch as ye are zealous of spiritual gifts, seek that ye may excel to the edifying of the church."

E- ENCOURAGE SOMEONE- It's better to get encouragement from someone than to encourage someone who is going through tough times. Sometimes you don't have any word to say or you don't know where to start. Using the right words to say and the issue of choice of words is 1 of the difficult things to do. Timing is another issue as you encourage a friend, church members or a counselee. To encourage someone in your circle or group means you're playing a team work. (Isaiah 41: 7) "So the carpenter encouraged the goldsmith, and he that smootheth with the hammer him that smote the anvil, saying, It is ready for the soldering: and he fastened it with nails, that it should not be moved."

SUNDAY- MI DAILY DEVOTION

MY HOSPITAL BED... JUST A BRIEF TESTIMONY OF GOD'S GRACE...

Before I gave you my brief testimony of the Lord's grace and mercy, let me share to you these beautiful verses from the Book of (Psalm 69:19- 20) 19- "Thou hast known my reproach, and my shame, and my dishonour: mine adversaries are all before thee. 20- Reproach hath broken my heart; and I am full of heaviness: and I looked for some to take pity, but there was none; and for comforters, but I found none."

I got up feeling great early Monday morning. I had my daily devotion and study. I went to the bank and went to church and do other things. I exercised and picked up my daughter. I went home and eat and made some phone calls and prepared for 2 meetings and then I felt something's wrong with my stomach, I felt some pain. I drove myself to the hospital which I don't really understand why I have abdominal pain. But I know God has always a purpose why He sent me to the hospital just like what He did in the past. While I was in the hospital, Mrs. Chit Miranda, one of the church members in Taylor started talking to me about this man (a patient in the hospital) who had a bad dream and it seems that it was about hell. In his dream, there was this bad spirit who tried to pull him to hell. This leads him to look for someone... someone whom he could talk to about God and the answer to his dream. Mrs. Miranda arranged the meeting with me for this man who was very disturbed and troubled. He came to my bed with so many questions and problems. One of his problems was fear and a troubled mind. He was a good and very religious person. I witnessed to him and talk to Him about the Lord and his destination. And to make the long story short, this man came to know the Lord in the hospital by my bed, while he was seated on his wheelchair.

And just before I left the hospital the next day, my wife and I visited him and prayed for him and saw tears in his eyes. Here's what he said before we left, "It's worth it, pastor; it's worth it..." He was talking about him being in the hospital and me being there too, because that leads to his salvation. He said that that day was the first time in his life that he slept so well and got up with a positive mind set and gratefulness. And he prayed that morning when he got up from bed. He said that all the garbage and rats in my head are gone. GOD IS AMAZING. He can use us even in our affliction and in our pain, in our sickness and in our weakness. Even in our trials or triumph. We just have to be willing to trust and obey. God can use you in whatever situations you are in right now, you must be willing to be used by God.

This is my wife's favorite verse as we commonly call it "My life verse..." (Nahum 1:7) "The LORD is good, a strong hold in the day of trouble; and he knoweth them that trust in him."

MONDAY- MI DAILY DEVOTION
(Luke 10: 38- 42)

"BUT ONE THING IS NEEDFUL…"

(Luke 10: 38- 42) 38- "Now it came to pass, as they went, that he entered into a certain village: and a certain woman named Martha received him into her house. 39- And she had a sister called Mary, which also sat at Jesus' feet, and heard his word. 40- But Martha was cumbered about much serving, and came to him, and said, Lord, dost thou not care that my sister hath left me to serve alone? bid her therefore that she help me. 41- And Jesus answered and said unto her, Martha, Martha, thou art careful and troubled about many things: 42- But one thing is needful: and Mary hath chosen that good part, which shall not be taken away from her."

The issue of differences is very obvious in our text. There are 2 different personalities, 2 different priorities and 2 different plans of 2 different people as recorded here. Although Martha and Mary were sisters, its shows by the way they treated Jesus that as 2 different people, they have different attitudes and characters. Their values, their visions in life and their views of things and people were different.

We have 4 children and we treat them differently and we deal with them in a different level. And the reasons for their differences were the same reasons as that of Mary and Martha… Martha was very caring while Mary was very attentive. Martha was so anxious of the physical things while Mary was more interested in spiritual things. Martha was active while Mary was more relaxed. Mary was more courteous, while Martha was very commanding and straight forward. Mary and Martha actually represent this present age Christians. We can see them in our homes and churches today. You can see yourself, your parents and siblings by their actions and by the way they conduct themselves in the presence of our Lord. "Priority" played a big role in this very special and historic event in the lives of Mary and Martha in the presence of our Lord. What is needful on Sundays? What is needful on your church events? What is needful in the work of the Lord? What is needful as you get up in the morning and before you go to bed? Put it first in your list and in your life.

Check out what Jesus said about the kind of person you could be just by looking at your fruits: (Matthew 7:15- 20) 15- "Beware of false prophets, which come to you in sheep's clothing, but inwardly they are ravening wolves. 16- Ye shall know them by their fruits…" (John 15:4- 5) 4- "Abide in me, and I in you. As the branch cannot bear fruit of itself, except it abide in the vine; no more can ye, except ye abide in me. 5- I am the vine, ye are the branches: He that abideth in me, and I in him, the same bringeth forth much fruit: for without me ye can do nothing."

TUESDAY- MI DAILY DEVOTION
(Acts 9: 4- 6)

PERSECUTIONS- IT'S ABOUT RELIGION, CULTURE, CONTROL OR MONEY…?

4- "And he fell to the earth, and heard a voice saying unto him, Saul, Saul, why persecutest thou me? 5- And he said, Who art thou, Lord? And the Lord said, I am Jesus whom thou persecutest: it is hard for thee to kick against the pricks. 6- And he trembling and astonished said, Lord, what wilt thou have me to do? And the Lord said unto him, Arise, and go into the city, and it shall be told thee what thou must do."

It was Sunday morning and I saw almost a hundred kids that were coming in into our small church in the Philippines. That was a very special day for God and everyone was excited and the church was loud and full of children and adults as well. There was this boy who was so closed to me during those times. He approached me with a smile and greeted me and he said, "Hello pastor Ely, good morning sir." And I remember touching the back of that boy as I responded to him and said, "Good morning." I can't remember his name, but I remember it very well, when he looked up to me and said, "Ouch! Pastor Ely, it hurts!" And I started asking some questions, but one of my Christian workers tapped me on my back and asked me if she could talk to me about the boy in private, so we did. We talked on the other side of the church and she said that the boy was being persecuted by his parents; meaning his parents doesn't want him to come to Sunday school and every time his parents finding him coming to church, they badly hit him with belt or stick on his back. Back then, the Philippines doesn't have a strict law or law against child abused. And if we have, it was not very well implemented because I, myself was physically abused by my dad when I was growing up. That was before my dad came to know the Lord Jesus Christ. We have the same problems going on right now on the other side of the globe. And let me call that *"family persecution"*. We have community persecution, persecution at work place, religious persecution and all kinds of persecutions, but I believe that the family persecution is one of the most painful kinds of persecution. Although physical persecution is really painful, but such persecution where they inflict pain on you can get healed in the process of time, but being persecuted by a family member, it really gets into your emotions, in your minds and nerves. I don't know how you could comprehend the reason behind such persecution, but if it's your own family who really hates you in the name of Christ, it's totally different. It was different with Apostle Paul before his encounter with the Lord Jesus Christ. Paul was a Pharisee and a religious leader, so I truly believe that Paul's persecution to the Christians before his conversion has something to do with his religious inclination and belief, as well as his religious position and what he will have to possess. How much and how long do you have to hate to convert someone to your religion and belief? And how much do you have to eliminate someone from his religion or religious belief so you can have control of every religion? That could be a good question for Apostle Paul when he persecuted the church of the Lord Jesus Christ. There's no doubt that the religious group where he belonged may have the same purpose and goals- take control like what the Romans did during those times. Politics and culture plays a big role in many persecutions all over the world. Just love them and pray for them, it sounds easy, but that's what they need. (Matthew 5:9-12). 9- "Blessed are the peacemakers: for they shall be called the children of God. 10- Blessed are they which are persecuted for righteousness' sake: for theirs is the kingdom of heaven. 11- Blessed are ye, when men shall revile you, and persecute you, and shall say all manner of evil against you falsely, for my sake. 12- Rejoice, and be exceeding glad: for great is your reward in heaven: for so persecuted they the prophets which were before you."

WEDNESDAY- MI DAILY DEVOTION
(Acts 9: 1- 3)

PAUL- A POLITICIAN AND THE PERSECUTOR

1- "And Saul, yet breathing out threatenings and slaughter against the disciples of the Lord, went unto the high priest, 2- And desired of him letters to Damascus to the synagogues, that if he found any of this way, whether they were men or women, he might bring them bound unto Jerusalem. 3- And as he journeyed, he came near Damascus: and suddenly there shined round about him a light from heaven: "

Paul was a Pharisee, a politician, a persecutor, a powerful man during his time and Paul was a men pleaser. Paul may only be four feet and a half in height. No wonder his name was Paul which means "Little", but his *arrogance*, his *accomplishment*, his *act of faith* and his dream was above his measure or his stature. Paul was born in Tarsus, a city of Cilicia, a free city of the Romans. Paul was from the tribe of Benjamin as according to some scholars. Paul called himself the Hebrew of the Hebrews. And it was obvious that Paul himself was a free man as a citizen of Rome, but he was a servant of sin and of Satan before his conversion. (Acts 9:1-2) 1- "And Saul, yet breathing out threatenings and slaughter against the disciples of the Lord, went unto the high priest, 2- And desired of him letters to Damascus to the synagogues, that if he found any of this way, whether they were men or women, he might bring them bound unto Jerusalem."

Paul in his breathed and in his life was out to harm, put in prison, destroy and kill the Christians. What an evil passion Paul has, but that was the truth. He was the persecutor of Christians. Paul obtained his great knowledge from the schools of Tarsus. He learned and earned his philosophy and poetry from the Greeks which during those times were one of the best or on the top. He was tutored under the feet of Gamaliel the Pharisee. In spite of his educational attainment, it did not hindered Paul from being the persecutor of the Christians and the church. But Paul had his greatest encounter in life. It was when he met the Lord Jesus Christ on his way to Damascus. Paul was busy on his persecution business, while God was there waiting to have a faced off with him. Paul was resisting the Lord. (Acts 9:4) "And he fell to the earth, and heard a voice saying unto him, Saul, Saul, why persecutest thou me?" Paul was knocking down Christians and kicking *God's work, God's way, God's workers and God's Word-The Bible.* (Acts 9:5) "And he said, Who art thou, Lord? And the Lord said, I am Jesus whom thou persecutest: it is hard for thee to kick against the pricks." Indeed, Paul was putting pressures on the Christians. He was not plowing off the field for God, but for himself and the religious Pharisees. But God made a turned around in the life of Saul of Tarsus. God turned around the table which made Saul who became Paul a changed man by the grace of God.

In (I Timothy 1:11-15) 11- "According to the glorious gospel of the blessed God, which was committed to my trust. 12- And I thank Christ Jesus our Lord, who hath enabled me, for that he counted me faithful, putting me into the ministry; 13- Who was before a blasphemer, and a persecutor, and injurious: but I obtained mercy, because I did it ignorantly in unbelief. 14- And the grace of our Lord was exceeding abundant with faith and love which is in Christ Jesus. 15- This is a faithful saying, and worthy of all acceptation, that Christ Jesus came into the world to save sinners; of whom I am chief."

THURSDAY- MI DAILY DEVOTION
(Leviticus 17:1-4)

THE PROCLAMATION OF THE LORD'S COMMAND

1- "And the LORD spake unto Moses, saying, 2- Speak unto Aaron, and unto his sons, and unto all the children of Israel, and say unto them; This is the thing which the LORD hath commanded, saying, 3- What man soever there be of the house of Israel, that killeth an ox, or lamb, or goat, in the camp, or that killeth it out of the camp, 4- And bringeth it not unto the door of the tabernacle of the congregation, to offer an offering unto the LORD before the tabernacle of the LORD; blood shall be imputed unto that man; he hath shed blood; and that man shall be cut off from among his people:"

Note how the Lord conveyed the message. First God spoke to Moses. Moses was the leader of the congregation of Israel. It's a good way of spreading the word by starting from the top to bottom. Also, if you want to do something or wanted to start a project, it's good to start communicating the project to the key people first. God started from Moses as recorded in verse 1-"And the LORD spake unto Moses, saying...," God wanted to communicate His commandments and He did it first- To Moses and then notice what God said in verse 2- "Speak unto Aaron, and unto his sons, and unto all the children of Israel, and say unto them; This is the thing which the LORD hath commanded, saying...,"

Moses- The top leader
Aaron- The High Priest
Aaron's sons- The priests
The Children of Israel- The common people.

In verses 3 and 4- "What man soever there be of the house of Israel, that killeth an ox, or lamb, or goat, in the camp, or that killeth it out of the camp, 4- And bringeth it not unto the door of the tabernacle of the congregation, to offer an offering unto the LORD before the tabernacle of the LORD; blood shall be imputed unto that man; he hath shed blood; and that man shall be cut off from among his people:"

During the Old Testament times, people were allowed to build an altar for them to offer sacrifices or offerings as they come to God for worship. It has to be a blood offering from the animals. If you remember Abraham and Noah, where-ever they were, they built an altar for their sacrifices to God. We can see here the importance of the command of God to Moses as it was very obvious on God chains of command. The command was very important and really needful for the Israelites to follow, because of the salvation it offers. The command can save the lives of the offender. And we all know that if it's the Lord's command, it must be obeyed and it serves its purpose for the good of humanity. In relation to the proclamation of the Lord's command, the second thing to consider would be the purpose of the Lord's command.

In the Book of (Leviticus 17:5-6) 5- "To the end that the children of Israel may bring their sacrifices, which they offer in the open field, even that they may bring them unto the LORD, unto the door of the tabernacle of the congregation, unto the priest, and offer them for peace offerings unto the LORD. 6- And the priest shall sprinkle the blood upon the altar of the LORD at the door of the tabernacle of the congregation, and burn the fat for a sweet savour unto the LORD."

FRIDAY- MI DAILY DEVOTION
(Proverbs 4:14-15)

"GOD'S WARNING"

14- "Enter not into the path of the wicked, and go not in the way of evil men. 15- Avoid it, pass not by it, turn from it, and pass away."

King Solomon the man who is full of wisdom warned us: 1) 1) Proverbs 4: 14 "Enter not into the path of the wicked… It's a warning for us not to enter into the gates of sin and practicing sinners. "Enter not"- The ticket to enter in into their path is free, but you have to pay for the consequences. Sin has a price tagged on it. Sin is like putting an ice cream on a cone or a cup with all the good things on the top of it, but you get all the bad things like sugar and cholesterol. Sin will make you laugh and happy for a moment, but will destroy and make your life miserable for eternity, unless you repent and ask God to forgive you of your sins. In (Proverbs 4: 15) Again King Solomon the man who is full of wisdom warned us: 2) "Avoid it…" The writer knows that going to the place of sinners is dangerous as you may get tempted as you enter into it. Not even to pass by it. How can we avoid sin when it's always in our path, before our eyes, in our home and it's just a click away from your couch or bed rooms. Our access to God has no difference with our access to sin and Satan's devices. Few reminders for every believer to know and remember so you will not fall into sin: 1) "Enter not…" It means we are not supposed to fellowship with sinners. What I mean of having fellowship with sinners is when you agree with their sinful acts. It's different when you are with sinners as compared to fellowshipping with sinners. We are all sinners in the sight of God. (Romans 3:10; 23) But the difference is when you have asked Christ to forgive you of your sins and you have repented of your sins. You are now a forgiven sinner before God and you're not living in sin but for God. While those who are still practicing sinners, their lives is still in sin and they are living in sin. Anyone who turned their back from God and would not repent of their sins; those are the people who lives in sin and their lifestyle are sinful in the sight of God. You don't walk along with them on their way to sin and Satan's devices. Apostle Paul put it this way in (II Corinthians 6:14-18). The Bible said that we "Enter not into the path of the wicked…" 2) "And go not in the way of evil men." When I was a pastor of a church in Subic, Philippines, I was told by a survival instructor for military about how to catch a monkey in the jungle. He said that the easiest way to catch a monkey is to set a trap. And the trap would be a coconut. He said that you make a small cut on the top of the coconut and scrape the white stuff or coconut meat and you may add some food or nuts in it. He said that once the monkey put his hand inside the coconut and got hold of the food on it, he'll never get loose of it and will run away holding onto the food with his hand closed. The monkey will then could not run fast or climb. It's very simple and interesting, but the lesson to learn in our analogy could be a life saving to many and beneficial even for eternity. It means be aware of the trap of the devil and don't step into its way to destruction. (Proverbs 28:18; 16:25) "Whoso walketh uprightly shall be saved: but he that is perverse in his ways shall fall at once." (II Peter 2:9) "The Lord knoweth how to deliver the godly out of temptations, and to reserve the unjust unto the day of judgment to be punished:" For Christians, the Lord promised us of deliverance according to Peter, but you have to live a godly life. He said, "The Lord knoweth how to deliver the godly out of temptations…" We need to be strong in the faith because Satan, our enemy is not taking a "time out" in his effort to deceive and destroy both Christians and his very own. Sometimes, Satan would start from a cookie in a cookie jar. He starts small to destroy big people, huge ministries and large amount of damages both in physical, financial, moral, emotional and spiritual life of a man or a woman. We know that prayer and the Word of God are our weapons against the wiles of the devil. We must use it to resist the enemy.

(I Peter 4:19) "Wherefore let them that suffer according to the will of God commit the keeping of their souls to him in well doing, as unto a faithful Creator."

SATURDAY- MI DAILY DEVOTION
(Romans 5:5-11)

THE LOVE OF GOD THE FATHER.

5- "And hope maketh not ashamed; because the love of God is shed abroad in our hearts by the Holy Ghost which is given unto us. 6- For when we were yet without strength, in due time Christ died for the ungodly. 7- For scarcely for a righteous man will one die: yet peradventure for a good man some would even dare to die. 8- But God commendeth his love toward us, in that, while we were yet sinners, Christ died for us. 9- Much more then, being now justified by his blood, we shall be saved from wrath through him. 10- For if, when we were enemies, we were reconciled to God by the death of his Son, much more, being reconciled, we shall be saved by his life. 11- And not only so, but we also joy in God through our Lord Jesus Christ, by whom we have now received the atonement."

"The LOVE of God is greater far than tongue or pen can ever tell. It goes beyond the highest star; and reaches to the lowest hell; the guilty pair, bowed down with care, God gave His Son to win. His erring child He reconciled and pardoned from sin. O love of God, how rich and pure! How measureless and strong! It shall forever more endure the saints' and angels song." (Frederick M. Lehman)

What a beautiful song. No one can measure, describe it in words or tongues and paint it in a canvas. Our mind is limited in its capacity to comprehend such LOVE. It's really beyond our human comprehension. Faith in the Lord and what He has done on the Cross two thousand years ago is the key to really understand His great love for humanity.

Only as if we "let" the Holy Spirit of God convicts us of our sins and our hopelessness and helplessness. Not only God showed us His love through His Son, God the Father was the one who executed such love on the Cross, no wonder when Jesus prayed in the garden of Gethsemane, He asked the Father to "…take this cup from me; yet not my will, but yours be done." (Luke 22: 42). The Lord Jesus Christ by His death on the Cross gave us the Father's love, and such love should serve us an example for us to follow. Let's explore the love of God in the Lord Jesus Christ.

In these Scripture verses, we have here the Lord's demonstration of His love for us. (John 3:16; I John 4: 7- 12). "For God so loved the world, that he gave his only begotten Son, that whosoever believeth in him should not perish, but have everlasting life." 7- "Beloved, let us love one another: for love is of God; and every one that loveth is born of God, and knoweth God. 8- He that loveth not knoweth not God; for God is love. 9- In this was manifested the love of God toward us, because that God sent his only begotten Son into the world, that we might live through him. 10- Herein is love, not that we loved God, but that he loved us, and sent his Son to be the propitiation for our sins. 11- Beloved, if God so loved us, we ought also to love one another. 12- No man hath seen God at any time. If we love one another, God dwelleth in us, and his love is perfected in us."

SUNDAY- MI DAILY DEVOTION
(John 3 16)

THE DEMONSTRATIONS OF GOD'S LOVE

"For God so loved the world, that he gave his only begotten Son, that whosoever believeth in him should not perish, but have everlasting life."

Can love be demonstrated in some ways beyond our understanding or comprehension? We all know that it can be and it has been demonstrated by people all over the world in many ways and formed. History reveals a long time ago about the king of India who spends millions of dollars to build the Taj mahal for the one he loves. That was an expensive demonstration of love in the human eyes. The story of love like Romeo and Juliet is one of the great love story ever written if not the greatest love story. Remember the movie of the 70's "The Love Story". This was a story of a man who remained faithful and true to his ailing wife. And you have your own love story and we can go on and on. But the greatest *demonstration of love* is at the Cross of Calvary. That was the greatest story ever told when God demonstrated His love on the Cross through the death of His Son for the sins of mankind. In (Romans 5:6) "For when we were yet without strength, in due time Christ died for the ungodly." In the midst of our hopelessness, our Holy God died for us. In verse 8 "But God commendeth his love toward us in that, while we were yet sinners, Christ died for us." So if you think that you can be saved because you are good and if you think you are holy, you are definitely wrong. You read what Romans 5: 8 says, "…while we were yet sinners…" and if you would look back to Romans 5: 6 it says that, "we are without strength and we are ungodly." We have nothing to boast of and nothing to be proud of. We are actually in a very desperate situation and condition. But the God of love and mercy demonstrated His love to us when we were without strength. You see, God created the whole world and the whole universe for us to enjoy. He created the trees, the mountains, the valleys and the seas for us to enjoy and yet we disobeyed Him. But in spite of our disobedience to Him, though He is a Holy God, He humbled himself and He died on the Cross for the propitiation of our sins. Jesus suffered and died because He loves us so much. (Hebrews 12: 1-2) "Looking unto Jesus, the author and finisher of our faith, who for the joy that was set before him endured the cross, despising the shame, and is set down at the right hand of the throne of God." Jesus endured the Cross and despised the shame for you and for me. He endured the suffering, the pain and the agony of the Cross. He despised the shame of being mocked and naked on the Cross and it's all because of His love for you and for me. Jesus took pride of taking our sins to himself. Millions of people around the world have watched "The Passion of the Christ" by Mel Gibson. It was very controversial for some reasons, but one of the controversial parts was the graphic scenes of the movie, which is not even as worst as if you picture it the way the Scriptures revealed the truth of what He went through. What a demonstration of a true and priceless love. Here's the unbelievable revelation and demonstration of the heart and mind of God in (Isaiah 53:10) "Yet it pleased the LORD to bruise him; he hath put him to grief: when thou shalt make his soul an offering for sin, he shall see his seed, he shall prolong his days, and the pleasure of the LORD shall prosper in his hand."

MONDAY- MI DAILY DEVOTION
(Deuteronomy 7:9; 13)

GOD THE FATHER WHO PLUGGED IN…

9- "Know therefore that the LORD thy God, he is God, the faithful God, which keepeth covenant and mercy with them that love him and keep his commandments to a thousand generations;" 13- "And he will love thee, and bless thee, and multiply thee: he will also bless the fruit of thy womb, and the fruit of thy land, thy corn, and thy wine, and thine oil, the increase of thy kine, and the flocks of thy sheep, in the land which he sware unto thy fathers to give thee."

In John 3:16 "For God so loved the world…" For those who read and speak Greek language, they may already have an idea of what I will be talking about. There are 3 different meaning for the word "world" in the Bible. 1- "World" as a claw- (Isaiah 40:22) " It is he that sitteth upon the circle of the earth, and the inhabitants thereof are as grasshoppers; that stretcheth out the heavens as a curtain, and spreadeth them out as a tent to dwell in:" (Psalms 24:1) "A Psalm of David. The earth is the LORD'S, and the fulness thereof; the world, and they that dwell therein." 2- "World" as a System- (Romans 12: 2) 2- "And be not conformed to this world: but be ye transformed by the renewing of your mind, that ye may prove what is that good, and acceptable, and perfect, will of God." 3- "World" as the whole humanity- (John 3:16) "For God so loved the world, that he gave his only begotten Son, that whosoever believeth in him should not perish, but have everlasting life."

We were created in His image and for His glory and we blew it off in the garden of Eden. Adam entertained Satan, listened to his voice and desired the tree of knowledge of good and evil (Genesis 2:9) and they fell into sin. What comes to your mind when you think of tragedies; we may think of 9/11 or the 2008 earthquake in China and the Katrina tragedy in New Orleans. But the tragedy of tragedies was in the Garden of Eden when men disobeyed God and fell into sin. The Book of (Isaiah 53: 6) "All we like sheep have gone astray; we have turned everyone to his own way, and the LORD hath laid on him the iniquity of us all."

I believe, if we could just picture what happened in the Garden of Eden after the fall of man, and the reaction of God after the fall and just imagine how it would look like after Adam and Eve sinned. I don't know how to really picture it in our little imagination. What would be your feeling if you've just made or invented an updated, most advanced and really high tech computer with everything on it, but there is only one restriction, it's only good for 110 volts. And your dearest friend or love ones plugged it in to 220 volts and you know what will happen next. That dearest friend or love ones not only blew off the most updated, most advanced and high tech computer, but could be his or her relationship with you as well. I remember last summer of 2007 when the whole family went to the Philippines for a vacation. I brought with me a CD player which was 110 volts. I gave it to my mother as a gift and my dearest mother was so excited and very grateful. I can still remember my mother's words as she was holding that black CD player in her hands… she said, (saying it in Visayan accent and dialect) "Thank God… now I can listen to my favorite Christian station". But my younger brother was more excited than my mother that he took the CD player from my mother's hand and plug it to 220 volts and "Bang!!!." My brother blew it off. It was plugged in into the wrong voltage.

Adam and Eve were plugged in into Satan's deception and in selfishness and sin, thus, they blew it off. By the way, my brother Joram went to be with the Lord, June 23, 2008 to be exact. I was at work when I received a call from my wife telling me that my sister AidaRiza from Subic, Zambales called and she needs money to go to Bacolod City for her airfare. I asked my wife why she (my sister) needs to go to our home town. My wife said: "Because Joram just passed away on his sleep." But the night before, my older brother Samson talked to him about spending a good vacation in Subic, Zambales. My brother Joram just received a good amount of money from my mother's insurance that was given to him as it was stated on her will. My good, humble and caring brother who took care of my mom and my dad physically and financially when they were alive said to my older brother Samson: "I'm not going to Subic, Zambales for a vacation; I'm going to heaven for a vacation…" And the night after that good conversation, Joram died in his sleep with his hands up like in a surrender position. Joram plugged in the wrong CD player in a wrong voltage, but I'm very much sure that Joram is plugged in to the right voltage in his spiritual life. Joram is plugged in to God where he is with right now. And not only for a vacation, but will be with our Lord forever. That's a perfect vacation with my dad, mom, and my brother Rev. Rosendo Sagansay, who was a faithful servant of the Lord, a good father and actually he was the one who got saved first in our family. Get plugged in with God right now. I remember what the Holy Scriptures said in (Acts 16:30-31) "And brought them out, and said, Sirs, what must I do to be saved?" In verse 31 it says, "And they said, Believe on the Lord Jesus Christ, and thou shalt be saved, and thy house."

TUESDAY- MI DAILY DEVOTION
(Titus 2:13)

IT IS YOUR BLESSED HOPE, LOOK FORWARD TO IT!!!

13- "Looking for that blessed hope, and the glorious appearing of the great God and our Saviour Jesus Christ;"

LOOKING- According to Webster's Dictionary means "To Direct the eye so as to see; To Gaze; To Consider; To expect; To Heed; To Face; To Appear; To See; To Express by a look."

HOPE- A Desire of some good, accompanied with a belief that it is attainable; Trust; One in whom trust or Confidence is placed; The object of hope; To Trust; To desire with some expectation of attainment." As according to Webster's Dictionary

Personal and relative duties must be done in obedience to his commands. We must aim at pleasing and honoring him as according to the Bible principles and commands. But we must also express our worship, love and duty to God by our belief and our fear and trust in Him. We must devote and dedicate ourselves to Him and Him alone by doing, obeying and observing all those religious duties and ordinances that the church has appointed. We must be in the spirit of prayer, praise and in constant meditation on God's Word and way. Godliness for me means to look up to God and claim Him and His Word to be true and faithful as you live according to what it says. There is no other way, but up. To go to God in any other way whether by saints or angels or priest is not only an insult to God, but a show of us ignoring His blessed hope. All communications from God to us are through his Son, and our returns must also be by him. It is of God in Christ that we must look at… as the object of our hope and worship. We need God, because our hope, our trust and our salvation in God were manifested in his Son. As the Lord looks down on us, preparing for his coming down here on earth; we as Christians ought to look up to Him with expectation of His coming which is the blessed hope for us Christians. It's so easy for us to look down, look at ourselves and to look on our sides than to look up to God. And by doing those, we sometimes made it hard for us while letting God's hand be upon us. (Hebrews 12:1- 2) 1- "Wherefore seeing we also are compassed about with so great a cloud of witnesses, let us lay aside every weight, and the sin which doth so easily beset us, and let us run with patience the race that is set before us, 2- Looking unto Jesus the author and finisher of our faith; who for the joy that was set before him endured the cross, despising the shame, and is set down at the right hand of the throne of God."

I like the Lord's promised in the Book of John as stated in (John 14:1-6) 1-"Let not your heart be troubled: ye believe in God, believe also in me. 2- In my Father's house are many mansions: if it were not so, I would have told you. I go to prepare a place for you. 3- And if I go and prepare a place for you, I will come again, and receive you unto myself; that where I am, there ye may be also. 4- And whither I go ye know, and the way ye know. 5- Thomas saith unto him, Lord, we know not whither thou goest; and how can we know the way? 6- Jesus saith unto him, I am the way, the truth, and the life: no man cometh unto the Father, but by me."

WEDNESDAY- MI DAILY DEVOTION
(II Chronicles 7:14)

CHRISTIANS FOR A FALLEN NATIONS

"If my people, which are called by my name, shall humble themselves, and pray, and seek my face, and turn from their wicked ways; then will I hear from heaven, and will forgive their sin, and will heal their land."

As we all know that this country and the whole world are all going through economic stress. The problem is some of the people out there would just blame the government for the problems. We have financial problems in this country and we also have moral and spiritual problems. And we have a problem that some people don't even care about. The problem that really affects millions of individuals, homes, churches and even businesses which I believe is the problem of the heart. The corrupt and deteriorated spiritual condition of man is one of the causes of the problems of many countries. People have a choice between God and Satan, between evil and good and between a country that will stand in righteousness or sin. (Proverbs 14:34) "Righteousness exalteth a nation, but sin is a reproach to any people." The politicians have the right to run for office as much as the citizen has the right to exercise their freedom to vote. But if you're a Christian, you will vote wisely and with wisdom and prudence as well as you will vote for someone who would set a good example and the one who lives a life that your son or daughter could be proud of. According to Hugh Pyle, "Historians reveals that fallen nations have first had a deep preoccupation with sex."

We either will stand for what is right and for revival or we will fall with those whose lives are wasted in sin and misery. You will either stand for God or you will just go with the flow. Have you ever been pulled over by a cop, because you were going 75 or 80 miles per hour on 45 miles per hour speed limit? And one of our invalid and unacceptable reasons is… "I'm going with the flow…" You are responsible for your decisions. You are responsible for this nation in bringing revival or decay. But as a believer and a father, I have to leave a legacy that my kids could look back and say; "Dad, you have done your best". We will do our best to save the spiritual distress and the moral decay of this country and the whole world. We can't win the whole world, but we can win our own small world. In order for us to have a revival in our country, in our churches or in our heart, Christians must take the challenge. Notice the Challenge of God to His people: "If my people which are called by my name shall humble themselves…" Take note of a saying in the Philippines: "Be humble lest you stumble." Those who live in sin and pride will soon live a defeated life. (Proverbs 16:19) "Better it is to be of an humble spirit with the lowly, than to devide the spoil with the proud." In humility of spirit, Christians should come to God in repentance and with a contrite heart. We must learn to trust the Lord for our church and for our community. We must learn not to trust in our own strength, but in the strength of the Lord. It's not by might nor by power, but by His Spirit. We sometimes trust in our own power and not in the power of God and in His Spirit. We trust in our own wisdom and not on the wisdom of God.

If you were called by His Name (God's name, In Jesus Name) the second challenge for us is to pray. One of the failures and weakness of many Christians is lack of prayer. Remember the story of Daniel during the time of Nebuchadnezzar in (Daniel 3). Nebuchadnezzar made a declaration or a law where people were commanded to worship the image that he made. And Daniel and the three young Hebrews refused to worship the god of Nebuchadnezzar. God will spare a nation, a home or an individual if we learn to pray to the living God. Remember during the time of Abraham when God talked to Abraham about God destroying Sodom and Gomorrah, because of their pride and immorality. (Genesis 18:20-33) And it's very unfortunate that we are going through the same problems in times like these. They went through the same problems when God warned Noah of the coming flood, it was the same problems and the only resolution to the problems is for us to cry out to God for our Nation, for our home and our churches. What's going on right now in every parts of the world should break our heart as we watch the lost and the Christians who have everything to enjoy, but spiritually empty. You notice what it says… "If my people…" It means "us" Christians.

(Ezekiel 22:30) "And I sought for a man among them, that should make up the hedge, and stand in the gap before me for the land, that I should not destroy it: but I found none."

THURSDAY- MI DAILY DEVOTION
(Genesis 13:1-12)

ARE YOU COMPETING OR GLORIFYING?

1- "And Abram went up out of Egypt, he, and his wife, and all that he had, and Lot with him, into the south.2- And Abram was very rich in cattle, in silver, and in gold.3- And he went on his journeys from the south even to Bethel, unto the place where his tent had been at the beginning, between Bethel and Hai; 4- Unto the place of the altar, which he had made there at the first: and there Abram called on the name of the LORD. 5- And Lot also, which went with Abram, had flocks, and herds, and tents. 6- And the land was not able to bear them, that they might dwell together: for their substance was great, so that they could not dwell together. 7- And there was a strife between the herdmen of Abram's cattle and the herdmen of Lot's cattle: and the Canaanite and the Perizzite dwelled then in the land. 8- And Abram said unto Lot, Let there be no strife, I pray thee, between me and thee, and between my herdmen and thy herdmen; for we be brethren. 9- Is not the whole land before thee? separate thyself, I pray thee, from me: if thou wilt take the left hand, then I will go to the right; or if thou depart to the right hand, then I will go to the left. 10- And Lot lifted up his eyes, and beheld all the plain of Jordan, that it was well watered every- where, before the LORD destroyed Sodom and Gomorrah, even as the garden of the LORD, like the land of Egypt, as thou comest unto Zoar. 11- Then Lot chose him all the plain of Jordan; and Lot journeyed east: and they separated themselves the one from the other. 12- Abram dwelled in the land of Canaan, and Lot dwelled in the cities of the plain, and pitched his tent toward Sodom."

We're having our 2010 Annual Filipino- American Sports Festival and Fellowship of Churches here in Michigan and as always, it would be great and fun. God has blessed us with so many talented young people and adults as well. The problems and the conflict between Abraham and Lot started when their influenced and wealth increased. It happens in many churches, organizations, in companies and homes. Conflicts, conflicts, conflicts!!! Jealousy, jealousy, jealousy!!! Envy, envy, envy!!! In the ministry, churches are filled with so many talents and smart members. We have good preachers and knowledgeable pastors. We have leaders with wisdom and information in their hearts and mind. We have churches and ministries that are doing well and others are not. We have people who are working hard and have given their lives for the work of the Lord and for the salvation of the lost. The success of an individual, church or ministry should be everyone's success as well, because we are in the same cause and serving the same God. Remember what David said when he confronted Goliath. (I Samuel 17:23- 29) "And as he talked with them, behold, there came up the champion, the Philistine of Gath, Goliath by name, out of the armies of the Philistines, and spake according to the same words: and David heard them. 24- And all the men of Israel, when they saw the man, fled from him, and were sore afraid. 25- And the men of Israel said, Have ye seen this man that is come up? surely to defy Israel is he come up: and it shall be, that the man who killeth him, the king will enrich him with great riches, and will give him his daughter, and make his father's house free in Israel. 28- "And Eliab his eldest brother heard when he spake unto the men; and Eliab's anger was kindled against David, and he said, Why camest thou down hither? and with whom hast thou left those few sheep in the wilderness? I know thy pride, and the naughtiness of thine heart; for thou art come down that thou mightest see the battle. 29- And David said, What have I now done? Is there not a cause?" His brother opposed him in his cause. Was it because of jealousy? Was it because of pride or sibling rivalry? Or his brother was anxious of what may happen to him and love him so much that he (Eliab) wants to keep him (David) away from harm. The conflict between David and Eliab is very obvious in this story. I suggest that the Mr. Eliab of this present time will just say the same words king Saul uttered as he sent David to do the job for him. King Saul parting words to David were… "Go, and the LORD be with thee." (I Samuel 17:37) "David said moreover, The LORD that delivered me out of the paw of the lion, and out of the paw of the bear, he will deliver me out of the hand of this Philistine. And Saul said unto David, Go, and the LORD be with thee." We have to work together, pray together, love each other and be in it together. If you remember the motto of the 3 musketeers *Athos, Porthos and Aramis,- inseparable friends who live by the motto* "All for one, One for all" *("tous pour un, un pour tous"* (The Bible Collection). Check out (Psalm 133:1- 3) 1- "A Song of degrees of David. Behold, how good and how pleasant it is for brethren to dwell together in unity! 2- It is like the precious ointment upon the head, that ran down upon the beard, even Aaron's beard: that went down to the skirts of his garments; 3- As the dew of Hermon, and as the dew that descended upon the mountains of Zion: for there the LORD commanded the blessing, even life for evermore."

FRIDAY- MI DAILY DEVOTION
(Matthew 14:24-33)

JESUS, WALKING ON THE SEA… *The Disciples knew His Voice…?*

24- "But the ship was now in the midst of the sea, tossed with waves: for the wind was contrary. 25- And in the fourth watch of the night Jesus went unto them, walking on the sea. 26- And when the disciples saw him walking on the sea, they were troubled, saying, It is a spirit; and they cried out for fear. 27- But straightway Jesus spake unto them, saying, Be of good cheer; it is I; be not afraid. 28- And Peter answered him and said, Lord, if it be thou, bid me come unto thee on the water. 29- And he said, Come. And when Peter was come down out of the ship, he walked on the water, to go to Jesus. 30- But when he saw the wind boisterous, he was afraid; and beginning to sink, he cried, saying, Lord, save me. 31- And immediately Jesus stretched forth his hand, and caught him, and said unto him, O thou of little faith, wherefore didst thou doubt? 32- And when they were come into the ship, the wind ceased. 33- Then they that were in the ship came and worshipped him, saying, Of a truth thou art the Son of God."

The closer we are with God the more the Holy Spirit reveals His love to us. The better we are able to deal with sin, Satan and our selfish motives. We shall be able to deal with our fears with God's help. Here in Michigan, there's a car insurance company that has an ads which says, "… You're in good hands." In my own observation, it speaks of security and their assurance to their consumers that if you're with them or sign in to them, you will be safe and secured. But it's just about your car insurance which is really just about money and coverage. We have God as our voice and security in times of needs.

It's also easier for us to accept our mistakes and failures. The Lord Jesus Christ in His grace helped the disciples when they were in trouble. Jesus is our good shepherd and we know Him. Perhaps the disciples fancied that it was some evil spirit that raised the storm. It is very common to many believers that most of the time, the problem of fear starts from the inside out. How these fears were silenced by the Lord was mentioned in verse 27- "Be of good cheer; it is I; be not afraid." He straightway relieved them, by showing them their mistake when they were having a hard time wrestling their fear and storms in life. Jesus did not mention His name as he did to Paul, because Paul was not a Christian during his encounter with Jesus. If I was there observing what was going on and just by listening to their conversations, I would assume that the disciples knew and recognized Him by His voice. When my son EJ got lost in a department store, I asked him "how did you find us? EJ said to me, "I heard your voice on the other aisle talking with mom, so I started looking for you over there…" After we found Him as our Savior and Lord, we recognized His voice already and know Him. It's an amazing spiritual blessing and grace from the Lord. (Jn. 10:4) "And when he putteth forth his own sheep, he goeth before them, and the sheep follow him: for they know his voice." (John 10:14; 27) "I am the good shepherd, and know my sheep, and am known of mine.27 My sheep hear my voice, and I know them, and they follow me:"

SATURDAY- MI DAILY DEVOTION
(Romans 1:9-10)

AS GOD'S CHILDREN; LET'S BE FAITHFUL IN OUR PRAYER LIFE.

9- "For God is my witness, whom I serve with my spirit in the gospel of his Son, that without ceasing I make mention of you always in my prayers; 10- Making request, if by any means now at length I might have a prosperous journey by the will of God to come unto you."

"Prayer and the Word of God are inseparable, and should always go together in the quiet time of the inner chamber." (Proverbs 28:9) "He that turneth away his ear from hearing the law, even his prayer shall be abomination."

"The churches are looking for better methods but God is looking for better men." What the church needs today is not more or better machinery, not new organizations or more methods, but men whom the Holy Ghost can use. Man of prayer, man mighty in prayer and man of God who will really love the Lord. The Holy Spirit does not flow though methods but through men. He does not come on machinery, but on men. He does not anoint plans, but men-men of prayer. Please don't get me wrong, I am for plans and machinery and goals, but the best of all is PRAY AND PRAY MORE for your plans, your goals and for the people involved. "Beginning the day with a devotional Bible study and prayer equips a man for the day's fight with self and sin and Satan." (John R. Mott)

Take note of this simple definition of P-R-A-Y; it means **P**lease the Lord, **R**eceive His **A**nswer and **Y**ield to His will.

I like this beautiful hymn about prayer.

In The Garden

I come to the garden alone
While the dew is still on the roses
And the voice I hear falling on my ear
The Son of God discloses.
And He walks with me, and He talks with me,
And He tells me I am His own;
And the joy we share as we tarry there,
None other has ever known.
He speaks, and the sound of His voice,
Is so sweet the birds hush their singing,
And the melody that He gave to me
Within my heart is ringing...
(Charles Austin Miles- 1912)

(Psalms 55:16-17) 16- "As for me, I will call upon God; and the LORD shall save me. 17- Evening, and morning, and at noon, will I pray, and cry aloud: and he shall hear my voice."

SUNDAY- MI DAILY DEVOTION
(Hebrews 11:5-6)

FAITH, YOUR FAITH…

5- "By faith Enoch was translated that he should not see death; and was not found, because God had translated him: for before his translation he had this testimony, that he pleased God. 6- But without faith it is impossible to please him: for he that cometh to God must believe that he is, and that he is a rewarder of them that diligently seek him."

In our Christian life, there are things that we need to put into practice and consistently live by them, which could be: FAITH in God, FELLOWSHIP with the believers, being consistent in FOLLOWING God's Word and way. Our hands are always full. We're always busy at home, at work, in our business and other things that sometimes don't really matter anymore. During the week or on week days, we set aside faith, fellowship with God and with our fellow believers. The worst is, even the Word of God and our duty and responsibilities as Christians are neglected at some point. Some people will see and notice how busy we are, but they don't seem to notice how faithful we are in the Lord. One of the sad things that can happen to the believers is if they don't see Christ in us. They don't see how we exercise our faith to God as Christians. Faith- you need faith in God for your salvation through the Lord Jesus Christ. Follow- you follow Christ's footsteps, commands and the Word of God. Fellowship- you develop a daily fellowship with God and with your fellow believers through Bible study and prayer.

PRESERVATION of our testimony is very important to us as the disciples of the Lord Jesus Christ. May it be at home, at work or at school, we must live the Christian life. We need to live in God's PRINCIPLES as stated in the Scriptures. We need to be consistent in PROCLAIMING the good news of salvation or the gospel of the Lord Jesus Christ. I like the song of Janet Paschal taken from the book of Romans which says: "I am not ashamed of the Gospel, the Gospel of Jesus Christ. I am not afraid to be counted, but I'm willing to give my life, see I'm ready to be, what He wants me to be, give up the wrong for the right, I am not ashamed of the Gospel…" Let us be more passionate for God, for His Word, in sharing the Word of God to the lost and be passionate to be like Jesus. We should have that readiness, revived spirit and re-focusing of our faith. Meditate on what Paul says in the Book of Romans and let it dig in into your heart. (Romans 1:15-16) 15- "So, as much as in me is, I am ready to preach the gospel to you that are at Rome also. 16- For I am not ashamed of the gospel of Christ: for it is the power of God unto salvation to every one that believeth; to the Jew first, and also to the Greek." We can also take the great words of Apostle Paul in the Book of (Romans 4: 18-21) 18- "Who against hope believed in hope, that he might become the father of many nations, according to that which was spoken, So shall thy seed be. 19-And being not weak in faith, he considered not his own body now dead, when he was about an hundred years old, neither yet the deadness of Sarah's womb: 20-He staggered not at the promise of God through unbelief; but was strong in faith, giving glory to God; 21- And being fully persuaded that, what he had promised, he was able also to perform."

MONDAY- MI DAILY DEVOTION
(Proverbs 16:3)

HOW TO START YOUR DAY WITH A POSITIVE ATTITUDE...

3- "Commit thy works unto the LORD, and thy thoughts shall be established."

1- Pray and read the Word of God (Holy Bible) before you start your daily routine. (Psalms 119:147-149) 147- "I prevented the dawning of the morning, and cried: I hoped in thy word. 148- Mine eyes prevent the night watches, that I might meditate in thy word. 149- Hear my voice according unto thy lovingkindness: O LORD, quicken me according to thy judgment."

2- Positive mind set, on the go spirit and trusting God's grace for the day. (Philippians 2:5) "Let this mind be in you, which was also in Christ Jesus:"

3- Peace of mind and the joy of the Lord is your strength. (Nehemiah 8:10) "Then he said unto them, Go your way, eat the fat, and drink the sweet, and send portions unto them for whom nothing is prepared: for this day is holy unto our Lord: neither be ye sorry; for the joy of the LORD is your strength."

4- Plan and prioritize your plan for the day. (Matthew 6:33) "But seek ye first the kingdom of God, and his righteousness; and all these things shall be added unto you."

5- Please God and encourage someone. (Colossians 3: 17; 23) 17- "And whatsoever ye do in word or deed, do all in the name of the Lord Jesus, giving thanks to God and the Father by him. 23- And whatsoever ye do, do it heartily, as to the Lord, and not unto men;"

6- *Purposely and prayerfully DO something significant.* (Philippians 4:1-8)

7- *Potentials and opportunities could be God's opened doors for you, grab it and step on it.* (Revelation 3:8) "I know thy works: behold, I have set before thee an open door, and no man can shut it: for thou hast a little strength, and hast kept my word, and hast not denied my name."

8- *Patiently, Let everything be done decently and in order.* Get it done in a right time and in a right way. (I Corinthians 14:40) "Let all things be done decently and in order."

9- *Problems are annoying and it will come. But set your focus to the right thing and the right Person- the Lord Jesus Christ.* (Hebrews 12:1-3) 1- "Wherefore seeing we also are compassed about with so great a cloud of witnesses, let us lay aside every weight, and the sin which doth so easily beset us, and let us run with patience the race that is set before us, 2- Looking unto Jesus the author and finisher of our faith; who for the joy that was set before him endured the cross, despising the shame, and is set down at the right hand of the throne of God. 3- For consider him that endured such contradiction of sinners against himself, lest ye be wearied and faint in your minds."

10- *Place everything into the hands of the living God...* It means that you have to entrust everything to God. (Proverbs 3:5-6) 5- "Trust in the LORD with all thine heart; and lean not unto thine own understanding. 6- In all thy ways acknowledge him, and he shall direct thy paths."

TUESDAY- MI DAILY DEVOTION
(Romans 4:1-5)

FAITH, STRONG AND TRUE FAITH

1- "What shall we say then that Abraham our father, as pertaining to the flesh, hath found? 2- For if Abraham were justified by works, he hath whereof to glory; but not before God. 3- For what saith the scripture? Abraham believed God, and it was counted unto him for righteousness. 4- Now to him that worketh is the reward not reckoned of grace, but of debt. 5- But to him that worketh not, but believeth on him that justifieth the ungodly, his faith is counted for righteousness."

As believers and disciples of the Lord Jesus Christ, it would be impossible for us to separate ourselves from the world systems since we're still in this world... but we can intentionally separate ourselves from the evil systems of this world. And it requires faith, strong and true faith. (II Corinthians 6:14-18) 14 "Be ye not unequally yoked together with unbelievers: for what fellowship hath righteousness with unrighteousness? and what communion hath light with darkness? 15- And what concord hath Christ with Belial? or what part hath he that believeth with an infidel? 16- And what agreement hath the temple of God with idols? for ye are the temple of the living God; as God hath said, I will dwell in them, and walk in them; and I will be their God, and they shall be my people. 17- Wherefore come out from among them, and be ye separate, saith the Lord, and touch not the unclean thing; and I will receive you, 18- And will be a Father unto you, and ye shall be my sons and daughters, saith the Lord Almighty."

It is wrong for believers to join with the wicked and profane. It is wrong and sinful to walk in their path or ways. The word unbeliever simply applies to all who don't trust in the saving grace of God. You really have to stand firm on what the Bible said about sin and wickedness. And we must know the difference between righteousness and unrighteousness, holiness and sinfulness. God will give us the grace to identify and to stand firm with our faith in Him, as we resist, oppose and stand against sin and sinfulness. We have to be strong in our faith and be consistent in our walk with God. Stand up for God and stand for what is right and pleasing to God. And it requires faith- strong and true faith. (Romans 5:1- 2) 1- "Therefore being justified by faith, we have peace with God through our Lord Jesus Christ: 2- By whom also we have access by faith into this grace wherein we stand, and rejoice in hope of the glory of God." We eat, we exercise and we rest and sleep so we can be physically fit and strong. We can do the same or more for our soul and for God. You read the Bible, you rest in God and you run the race and fight a good fight of faith. Fitness guru Jack Lalanne once said, "The only way you can hurt the body is not use it." LaLanne's workout show was a television staple from the 1950s to '70s. He maintained a youthful physique into his 80s."- Yahoo news. Listen and meditate to what Paul said in his letter to the believers during his time. We can claim the same victory in Christ Jesus our Lord. (I Corinthians 15:57) "But thanks be to God, which giveth us the victory through our Lord Jesus Christ."

WEDNESDAY- MI DAILY DEVOTION
(Romans 10:8-17)

FAITH + CONVERSION = SALVATION?

8- "But what saith it? The word is nigh thee, even in thy mouth, and in thy heart: that is, the word of faith, which we preach; 9- That if thou shalt confess with thy mouth the Lord Jesus, and shalt believe in thine heart that God hath raised him from the dead, thou shalt be saved. 10- For with the heart man believeth unto righteousness; and with the mouth confession is made unto salvation. 11- For the scripture saith, Whosoever believeth on him shall not be ashamed. 12- For there is no difference between the Jew and the Greek: for the same Lord over all is rich unto all that call upon him. 13- For whosoever shall call upon the name of the Lord shall be saved. 14- How then shall they call on him in whom they have not believed? and how shall they believe in him of whom they have not heard? and how shall they hear without a preacher? 15- And how shall they preach, except they be sent? as it is written, How beautiful are the feet of them that preach the gospel of peace, and bring glad tidings of good things! 16- But they have not all obeyed the gospel. For Esaias saith, Lord, who hath believed our report? 17- So then faith cometh by hearing, and hearing by the word of God."

FAITH starts from CONVERSION. It should start from knowing God in your heart. It does not start from the religion you were born in; neither will it start from your tradition and culture. To be born again or to be a Christian does not start from what you have learned from the past, in your religious experienced, but in your personal experience with the Lord Jesus Christ. (Matthew 13:15; 18:3). Paul conversion or testimony as recorded in (Galatians 1: 11-14). 11- "But I certify you, brethren, that the gospel which was preached of me is not after man. 12- For I neither received it of man, neither was I taught it, but by the revelation of Jesus Christ. 13- For ye have heard of my conversation in time past in the Jews' religion,how that beyond measure I persecuted the church of God, and wasted it: 14- And profited in the Jews' religion above many my equals in mine own nation, being more exceedingly zealous of the traditions of my fathers." First of all, as Paul testified that the gospel was preached to him and that was not of man. As the head of Jewish religion and a persecutor, Paul heard Stephen preached as recorded in Acts chapters 6 and 7.

The Apostle Paul said in (Romans 10:17) "So then faith cometh by hearing, and hearing by the word of God." It means that conversion starts from knowing Christ as your Lord and Savior. It's not a change of religion, but a change of a relationship. The Lord has changed our relationship from Satan to God as our Father, Savior, Lord and King. (John 8:44; 1:12) It's not a change of personality, but a change in a person, a change of heart. (II Corinthians 5:17). So FAITH gives us life, hope, peace and a home in heaven. And it also gives us a new position, possession and abundant life. (John 10:9-10) "I am the door: by me if any man enter in, he shall be saved, and shall go in and out, and find pasture. 10- The thief cometh not, but for to steal, and to kill, and to destroy: I am come that they might have life, and that they might have it more abundantly."

THURSDAY- MI DAILY DEVOTION
(Romans 10:8-17)

FROM CONVERSION TO CONVICTION

8- "But what saith it? The word is nigh thee, even in thy mouth, and in thy heart: that is, the word of faith, which we preach; 9- That if thou shalt confess with thy mouth the Lord Jesus, and shalt believe in thine heart that God hath raised him from the dead, thou shalt be saved. 10- For with the heart man believeth unto righteousness; and with the mouth confession is made unto salvation. 11- For the scripture saith, Whosoever believeth on him shall not be ashamed. 12- For there is no difference between the Jew and the Greek: for the same Lord over all is rich unto all that call upon him. 13- For whosoever shall call upon the name of the Lord shall be saved. 14- How then shall they call on him in whom they have not believed? and how shall they believe in him of whom they have not heard? and how shall they hear without a preacher? 15- And how shall they preach, except they be sent? as it is written, How beautiful are the feet of them that preach the gospel of peace, and bring glad tidings of good things! 16- But they have not all obeyed the gospel. For Esaias saith, Lord, who hath believed our report? 17- So then faith cometh by hearing, and hearing by the word of God."

Paul's conversion in (Acts 9:1-18) leads to CONVICTION. (John 16:8-9) 8- "And when he is come, he will reprove the world of sin, and of righteousness, and of judgment: 9- Of sin, because they believe not on me;" (Romans 8:13-16) 13- "For if ye live after the flesh, ye shall die: but if ye through the Spirit do mortify the deeds of the body, ye shall live. 14- For as many as are led by the Spirit of God, they are the sons of God. 15- For ye have not received the spirit of bondage again to fear; but ye have received the Spirit of adoption, whereby we cry, Abba, Father. 16- The Spirit itself beareth witness with our spirit, that we are the children of God:" As a new believer, you will start to feel and look at sin differently. You will begin to have a different perspective after you came to know the Lord and you will have a different conviction about sin. Keep in mind that no one will always be there for you but God. Your pastor and mentor will not always be there all the time to guide and convict you. They would not even be there to serve as a conscience to you. But praise God! We have the Holy Spirit who will always be there for us. Something really great happened to us the day we came to know the Lord. It's something that we cannot explain the miracle of a changed life. The conviction of the Holy Spirit is something that is beyond our imagination. It's something that your parents, friends and even your own wisdom, knowledge and strength can't do, but by His Holy Spirit.

Let's meditate on the revelation of the Lord Jesus Christ to Apostle John by the leading of the Holy Spirit of God. (John 14:26; 16:13-14) 26- "But the Comforter, which is the Holy Ghost, whom the Father will send in my name, he shall teach you all things, and bring all things to your remembrance, whatsoever I have said unto you." 13- "Howbeit when he, the Spirit of truth, is come, he will guide you into all truth: for he shall not speak of himself; but whatsoever he shall hear, that shall he speak: and he will show you things to come. 14- He shall glorify me: for he shall receive of mine, and shall show it unto you."

FRIDAY- MI DAILY DEVOTION
(Romans 10:8-17)

WE WERE SAVED TO COMMIT AND STAND FOR GOD

8- "But what saith it? The word is nigh thee, even in thy mouth, and in thy heart: that is, the word of faith, which we preach; 9- That if thou shalt confess with thy mouth the Lord Jesus, and shalt believe in thine heart that God hath raised him from the dead, thou shalt be saved. 10- For with the heart man believeth unto righteousness; and with the mouth confession is made unto salvation. 11- For the scripture saith, Whosoever believeth on him shall not be ashamed. 12- For there is no difference between the Jew and the Greek: for the same Lord over all is rich unto all that call upon him. 13- For whosoever shall call upon the name of the Lord shall be saved. 14- How then shall they call on him in whom they have not believed? and how shall they believe in him of whom they have not heard? and how shall they hear without a preacher? 15- And how shall they preach, except they be sent? as it is written, How beautiful are the feet of them that preach the gospel of peace, and bring glad tidings of good things! 16- But they have not all obeyed the gospel. For Esaias saith, Lord, who hath believed our report? 17- So then faith cometh by hearing, and hearing by the word of God."

Commitment is not a very popular word today whether at home, church or in some relationship. Yes, in your own family, in your own relationship with your parents or in your own relationship with your children. Do we have a firm commitment for God and love ones? There are people out there in a boyfriend- girlfriend relationship and yet, they don't want to get married for lack of commitment. Be sure to set your heart right with God and with the one you love. We also need commitment in our service for our church. Would you be willing to make a commitment for your home church or ministry? Be sure to strengthen your relationship with our Lord and Savior.

We need people who are willing to commit and dedicate their lives to God and the ministry. We need men and women who have a heart for God and for His glory. (Romans 12:1-2) "I beseech you therefore, brethren, by the mercies of God, that ye present your bodies a living sacrifice, holy, acceptable unto God, which is your reasonable service. 2- And be not conformed to this world: but be ye transformed by the renewing of your mind, that ye may prove what is that good, and acceptable, and perfect, will of God." Jesus said, "But seek ye first the kingdom of God…" It means that we must make His kingdom our focus and priority. We have to be kingdom focus. As one preacher said, "Make it be (God's Kingdom) your business…" If we make God's kingdom our priority, then we will have His provision and if we make God's righteousness our passion, then we will have His providence. Jesus first before anybody else and be willing to be counted for Him. Christ must be first in everything and everyone. When the poor widow put God and His Word first in her needs and in her life, the Lord honored her faithfulness. (I Kings 17:8- 16) When the women in (II Kings 4:1- 37) honored the Lord and His Word, God blessed them more than their expectations. They stood up tall for His Word and His honor and glory. (Ezekiel 22:30) "And I sought for a man among them, that should make up the hedge, and stand in the gap before me for the land, that I should not destroy it: but I found none."

SATURDAY- MI DAILY DEVOTION
(Luke 9: 56- 62)

COMMITMENT IS ABOUT DEDICATION AND SACRIFICES

56- "For the Son of man is not come to destroy men's lives, but to save them. And they went to another village. 57- And it came to pass, that, as they went in the way, a certain man said unto him, Lord, I will follow thee whithersoever thou goest. 58- And Jesus said unto him, Foxes have holes, and birds of the air have nests; but the Son of man hath not where to lay his head. 59- And he said unto another, Follow me. But he said, Lord, suffer me first to go and bury my father. 60- Jesus said unto him, Let the dead bury their dead: but go thou and preach the kingdom of God. 61- And another also said, Lord, I will follow thee And Jesus said unto him, No man, having put his hand to the plow, and looking back, is fit for the kingdom of God.; but let me first go bid them farewell, which are at home at my house. 62- And Jesus said unto him, No man, having put his hand to the plow, and looking back, is fit for the kingdom of God."

When you talk about *commitment*, it means you're talking about dedication, devotion, sacrifices, selfless desire and unconditional love. That's what it means to commit your life for the cause of Christ, your family or relationship. When King David stood and fought against Goliath and even before his encounter with Goliath, we can see David's commitment already not only in his family, but also in God as recorded in (I Samuel 17:20; 28-29) 20- "And David rose up early in the morning, and left the sheep with a keeper, and took, and went, as Jesse had commanded him; and he came to the trench, as the host was going forth to the fight, and shouted for the battle. 28- And Eliab his eldest brother heard when he spake unto the men; and Eliab's anger was kindled against David, and he said, Why camest thou down hither? and with whom hast thou left those few sheep in the wilderness? I know thy pride, and the naughtiness of thine heart; for thou art come down that thou mightest see the battle. 29- And David said, What have I now done? Is there not a cause?" Every Christian has all the reasons to serve and be committed to the one who gave His life for all. It means "no turning back, no turning back..." (Luke 9: 62) "And Jesus said unto him, No man, having put his hand to the plow, and looking back, is fit for the kingdom of God." We have all the reasons to be committed to the cause of Christ. For King David, he was willing to stand on the danger zone and kill Goliath without money involved and even with opposition. He was willing to kill the enemy of God for free. Now, that's commitment!!! Let me share to you 7 ways to serve the Lord: 1- Serve God from where you are 2- Serve Him for Who God is and what you have. 3- Serve God in whatever situation you are in right now. 4- Serve the Lord with what you have in your hands. 5- Serve the Lord by being a good parent, son or daughter... 6- You can serve God with your talents, time and treasures. 7- Serve God faithfully and with sincerity. (Joshua 24:21-22) 21- "And the people said unto Joshua, Nay; but we will serve the LORD. 22- And Joshua said unto the people, Ye are witnesses against yourselves that ye have chosen you the LORD, to serve him. And they said, We are witnesses." Listen to Paul's testimony from the Book of (Galatians 2:20) "I am crucified with Christ: nevertheless I live; yet not I, but Christ liveth in me: and the life which I now live in the flesh I live by the faith of the Son of God, who loved me, and gave himself for me."

SUNDAY- MI DAILY DEVOTION
(Matthew 10:1-6)

"COMMITMENT…"- NOT A COMMON WORD

1- "And when he had called unto him his twelve disciples, he gave them power against unclean spirits, to cast them out, and to heal all manner of sickness and all manner of disease. 2- Now the names of the twelve apostles are these; The first, Simon, who is called Peter, and Andrew his brother; James the son of Zebedee, and John his brother; 3- Philip, and Bartholomew; Thomas, and Matthew the publican; James the son of Alphaeus, and Lebbaeus, whose surname was Thaddaeus; 4- Simon the Canaanite, and Judas Iscariot, who also betrayed him. 5- These twelve Jesus sent forth, and commanded them, saying, Go not into the way of the Gentiles, and into any city of the Samaritans enter ye not: 6- But go rather to the lost sheep of the house of Israel."

Let me share to you the short outline from our text from Matthew chapter 10. 1- The Commission of the Disciples. 2- The Command to the Disciples. 3- The Commitment of the Disciples.

The Lord Jesus Christ ordained the disciples to preach the Word to all people. He called them individually to be a witness of Christ and His gift of salvation. He commissioned them to rebuke and stand against the evil and unclean spirits, to heal all manner of sicknesses and to preach the good tidings of great joy. Jesus sent them forth and He commanded them to "GO". And without the Lord's grace and hand upon them and their commitment as the Lord's disciples… they could never have turned the world upside down. As the disciples of the Lord Jesus Christ, they were trained and have learned from God and His Word. Christ Himself commissioned and ordained them for the greatest job and ministry on earth, which is the preaching of His Word. The ministry was and still is the greatest thing from heaven and was entrusted to the disciples for them to make the best out of it. And they were tried and tested. And it was not, and did not, and will not come easy. They were trained to be disciplined and faithful. (Matthew 10:16) "Behold, I send you forth as sheep in the midst of wolves: be ye therefore wise as serpents, and harmless as doves." Some Christians, they have a misconception and different mindset when it comes to serving God. Some religious organizations would sometimes think that serving God would mean pastorate or mission work at home or overseas. Some religious groups, their leaders would ask them to do things that are beyond our imaginations as their proof of their love and service to God. Some were trained to be a warrior, while other religious organizations are training their converts and send them to foreign missions to be missionaries in their own expense.

Paul's invitation to Christians in (Romans 12:1- 2) 1- "I beseech you therefore, brethren, by the mercies of God, that ye present your bodies a living sacrifice, holy, acceptable unto God, which is your reasonable service. 2- And be not conformed to this world: but be ye transformed by the renewing of your mind, that ye may prove what is that good, and acceptable, and perfect, will of God."

MONDAY- MI DAILY DEVOTION
(Matthew 10:7-14)

CHRIST'S COMMAND IS TO *"GO"*

7- "And as ye go, preach, saying, The kingdom of heaven is at hand. 8- Heal the sick, cleanse the lepers, raise the dead, cast out devils: freely ye have received, freely give. 9- Provide neither gold, nor silver, nor brass in your purses, 10- Nor scrip for your journey, neither two coats, neither shoes, nor yet staves: for the workman is worthy of his meat. 11- And into whatsoever city or town ye shall enter, inquire who in it is worthy; and there abide till ye go thence. 12- And when ye come into an house, salute it. 13- And if the house be worthy, let your peace come upon it: but if it be not worthy, let your peace return to you. 14- And whosoever shall not receive you, nor hear your words, when ye depart out of that house or city, shake off the dust of your feet.

It is written in the Book of (Luke 8:1) that Jesus went out to preach with His twelve disciples. He preached in every city and village and showing them the glad tidings of the kingdom of God. It is very obvious that Jesus was not only showing and training His disciples how to witness and tell others about the good news of the kingdom, but He was also trying to set a good example to them. Now Jesus in (Matthew 10:7), He was giving them the command to GO. "And as ye go, preach, saying, The kingdom of heaven is at hand." In verse 7 Christ told them that preaching of His Word was their main or primary objective, while in verse 8 are their secondary objective. Notice the next four objectives of Jesus. Jesus started talking to them about doing such things as: Healing..., Cleansing..., Raising... and Casting... I believe with all my heart that God is still in those businesses. The preaching and other ministries mentioned in verse 8 are just part of the greater vision and ministries that God had in stored for His children. I just don't know how many pastors, missionaries and lay people who are really committed in doing such things for the kingdom of heaven. We were saved to do God's business and be faithful and committed to our calling as servants of Christ. Would you be willing to preach the gospel and heal the sick… and be faithful to everything that God had entrusted to you with integrity, honesty, dignity and with the love of the Lord and for His people? We were told to follow Him in whatever situations we are in, whatever hardship we're going through and what the future may look like to you. Following Jesus in His way, in His work and by His Word will not be according to our own timing, title or will not be based on how much treasures we have. God wanted for us to follow His footsteps and His will no matter what's going on in our life, right now. (Matthew 8: 19- 23) 19- "And a certain scribe came, and said unto him, Master, I will follow thee whithersoever thou goest. 20- And Jesus saith unto him, The foxes have holes, and the birds of the air have nests; but the Son of man hath not where to lay his head. 21- And another of his disciples said unto him, Lord, suffer me first to go and bury my father. 22- But Jesus said unto him, Follow me; and let the dead bury their dead. 23- And when he was entered into a ship, his disciples followed him." (I Corinthians 10:31-33) "Whether therefore ye eat, or drink, or whatsoever ye do, do all to the glory of God. 32- Give none offence, neither to the Jews, nor to the Gentiles, nor to the church of God: 33- Even as I please all men in all things, not seeking mine own profit, but the profit of many, that they may be saved."

TUESDAY- MI DAILY DEVOTION
(Matthew 10:7-14)

THE DISCIPLES COMMITMENT TO THE KINGDOM

7- "And as ye go, preach, saying, The kingdom of heaven is at hand. 8- Heal the sick, cleanse the lepers, raise the dead, cast out devils: freely ye have received, freely give. 9- Provide neither gold, nor silver, nor brass in your purses, 10- Nor scrip for your journey, neither two coats, neither shoes, nor yet staves: for the workman is worthy of his meat. 11- And into whatsoever city or town ye shall enter, inquire who in it is worthy; and there abide till ye go thence. 12- And when ye come into an house, salute it. 13- And if the house be worthy, let your peace come upon it: but if it be not worthy, let your peace return to you. 14- And whosoever shall not receive you, nor hear your words, when ye depart out of that house or city, shake off the dust of your feet."

Evangelism is about sharing Jesus. Christians should do it more than just a habit or like a habit. Christians should do it more than just a lifestyle, but it's should be your life and joy. It's like drinking water every after meal, drinking coffee in the morning or drinking something hot to start your day. If you want to complain about the hardships that you're going through right now as a Christian, I want for you to consider this first before you complain. Notice what happened to the disciples for preaching and standing for God and for staying faithful unto the end. 1- Philip was scourged and he was crucified. 2- Matthew was nailed to the ground with spikes and he was beheaded. 3- Simon was tortured and he also was crucified upside down. 4- John the son of Zebedee was also tortured and was in exiled. 5- James the brother of John was beheaded. The twelve disciples of the Lord Jesus Christ in the New Testament suffered cruel torture and pain and even death for the sake of the gospel and of the Lord Jesus Christ. They stood up on their convictions and preached that Jesus is God, He's alive and He's the King of kings and the Lord of lords. Let me share to you some of the reasons why they were able to sacrificed and gave their life for the sake of the gospel: 1- Because of the grace of God that was in them 2- Because of their love for the Lord 3- Because they remained faithful and true 4- Because of their commitment and 5- Because they were looking forward for that day in heaven where God would say to them, "… Well done, thou good and faithful servant: thou hast been faithful over a few things, I will make thee ruler over many things: enter thou into the joy of thy lord." (Matthew 25:21). 6- Because they were looking forward of that crowning day in heaven.

(II Timothy 4: 5) "But watch thou in all things, endure afflictions, do the work of an evangelist, make full proof of thy ministry. 6- For I am now ready to be offered, and the time of my departure is at hand. 7- I have fought a good fight, I have finished my course, I have kept the faith: 8- Henceforth there is laid up for me a crown of righteousness, which the Lord, the righteous judge, shall give me at that day: and not to me only, but unto all them also that love his appearing."

WEDNESDAY- MI DAILY DEVOTION
(II Timothy 4:1-8)

CHRIST'S COMMAND... THE APOSTLE PAUL'S COMMITMENT...

1- "I charge thee therefore before God, and the Lord Jesus Christ, who shall judge the quick and the dead at his appearing and his kingdom; 2- Preach the word; be instant in season, out of season; reprove, rebuke, exhort with all longsuffering and doctrine. 3- For the time will come when they will not endure sound doctrine; but after their own lusts shall they heap to themselves teachers, having itching ears; 4- And they shall turn away their ears from the truth, and shall be turned unto fables. 5- But watch thou in all things, endure afflictions, do the work of an evangelist, make full proof of thy ministry. 6- For I am now ready to be offered, and the time of my departure is at hand. 7- I have fought a good fight, I have finished my course, I have kept the faith: 8- Henceforth there is laid up for me a crown of righteousness, which the Lord, the righteous judge, shall give me at that day: and not to me only, but unto all them also that love his appearing."

The work of the minister of the gospel is unique and very special in the sight of God and may not be as pleasing to others who have no hope. But Christians should know and understand that witnessing as commonly known as soul winning or evangelism was ordained and was entrusted to every believer of the Lord Jesus Christ. We can tell the importance of spreading the good news of salvation by the Lord's command. When He gave us the great commission to *"GO"* as according to (Matthew 28:18-20), He expect us to *GO*. But the Apostle Paul has a warning for us Christians in (I Corinthians 9:16-18) 16- "For though I preach the gospel, I have nothing to glory of: for necessity is laid upon me; yea, woe is unto me, if I preach not the gospel!" If you are a Christian, you are Christ's minister and as a minister of the gospel of the Lord Jesus Christ, we are required to be faithful in the business of preaching the gospel. 17- "For if I do this thing willingly, I have a reward: but if against my will, a dispensation of the gospel is committed unto me. 18- What is my reward Then? Verily that, when I preach the gospel, I may make the gospel of Christ without charge, that I abuse not my power in the gospel." The Lord by His grace entrusted to us the preaching of the gospel. He wants for us to be faithful and committed to His command to *GO*. And not everyone we get in contact with or shared with will agree on our message. We cannot question Apostle Paul's love, dedication, commitment to God and His Word and his sacrifices for the gospel of the Lord Jesus Christ. He has given not just his life but his everything. He did not withhold anything for our Lord and for the Lord's work. I wonder how many Christians out there who can't even give their small and little things for God or surrender that little stuff that hindered them from serving and being committed to Him. (I Corinthians 1: 17- 19) 17- "For Christ sent me not to baptize, but to preach the gospel: not with wisdom of words, lest the cross of Christ should be made of none effect. 18- For the preaching of the cross is to them that perish foolishness; but unto us which are saved it is the power of God. 19- For it is written, I will destroy the wisdom of the wise, and will bring to nothing the understanding of the prudent." Paul's warning was "woe unto him who preach not the gospel."

THURSDAY- MI DAILY DEVOTION
(II Timothy 4:1-8)

THE APOSTLE PAUL'S COMMITMENT TO GOD IS UNQUESTIONABLE

1- "I charge thee therefore before God, and the Lord Jesus Christ, who shall judge the quick and the dead at his appearing and his kingdom; 2- Preach the word; be instant in season, out of season; reprove, rebuke, exhort with all longsuffering and doctrine. 3- For the time will come when they will not endure sound doctrine; but after their own lusts shall they heap to themselves teachers, having itching ears; 4- And they shall turn away their ears from the truth, and shall be turned unto fables. 5- But watch thou in all things, endure afflictions, do the work of an evangelist, make full proof of thy ministry. 6- For I am now ready to be offered, and the time of my departure is at hand. 7- I have fought a good fight, I have finished my course, I have kept the faith: 8- Henceforth there is laid up for me a crown of righteousness, which the Lord, the righteous judge, shall give me at that day: and not to me only, but unto all them also that love his appearing."

As Christians and preachers, we are to preach the plain and purely Word of God and not ourselves or other people's lives. The Word of God is being abused and used for personal gain and interests and the Bible is being changed and corrupted. The truth of the gospel of the Lord Jesus Christ is not being shared with honesty. God expects every Christians to do so. (John 6:63) "It is the spirit that quickeneth; the flesh profiteth nothing: the words that I speak unto you, they are spirit, and they are life." We have the truth and we know the truth, but we sometimes just take the truth for granted and don't even dare to share the truth of the gospel. Jesus wants for us to be truthful and be intentional in sharing the Word of God. Even in His deepest moment, Jesus shared the truth to Pilate and those who were with him. (John 18:37-38) 37- "Pilate therefore said unto him, Art thou a king then? Jesus answered, Thou sayest that I am a king. To this end was I born, and for this cause came I into the world, that I should bear witness unto the truth. Every one that is of the truth heareth my voice. 38- Pilate saith unto him, What is truth? And when he had said this, he went out again unto the Jews, and saith unto them, I find in him no fault at all." You have heard of people sharing both their good and bad experiences on hotels, department stores, restaurants and their bad experiences in their trips or with people. You have heard of people telling their friends with excitement about the sale in a store or the good deals they got from garage sale. It's sad to say that some Christians were hesitant to share the Word of God to their friends or love ones. Many don't even dare to share the good news by just giving them the gospel tracts. We should be more excited to share to them about eternity than those things that are temporary and worldly. (I Corinthians 1: 21- 25) 21- "For after that in the wisdom of God the world by wisdom knew not God, it pleased God by the foolishness of preaching tosave them that believe. 22- For the Jews require a sign, and the Greeks seek after wisdom: 23-But we preach Christ crucified, unto the Jews a stumblingblock, and unto the Greeks foolishness; 24- But unto them which are called, both Jews and Greeks, Christ the power of God, and the wisdom of God. 25- Because the foolishness of God is wiser than men; and the weakness of God is stronger than men."

FRIDAY MI DAILY DEVOTION
(I Peter 4:5- 8)

"KEEP WATCHING"

5- "Who shall give account to him that is ready to judge the quick and the dead. 6- For for this cause was the gospel preached also to them that are dead, that they might be judged according to men in the flesh, but live according to God in the spirit. 7- But the end of all things is at hand: be ye therefore sober, and watch unto prayer. 8- And above all things have fervent charity among yourselves: for charity shall cover the multitude of sins."

When you come to the Lord, He will never send you away and He will not let His children come to Him and leave empty unless you come to Him with doubt in your heart.

Waeccan, - keep watch, to be awake, wacian-to be awake, it's where the word "wake" came from. This word is basically means "Keeping watch by night" as a form of protection.

The believers have common responsibilities. As God's children we need to WATCH: *WE MUST WATCH OUR HEART.* The meaning of heart: 1- The physical heart; 2- The spiritual heart. It is the heart that responds to God as you come to Him for repentance and faith. For example: If you will come to God right now in repentance and faith, asking him to forgive you of your sins. It involves: 1- The intellectual element. "This implies a change of view. It is a change of view with regard to sin, God and self. Sin comes to be recognized as personal guilt. God is the one who justly demands righteousness and self as defiled and helpless. (Romans 3:20) "Therefore by the deeds of the law there shall no man be justified in the sight in his sight: for by the law is the knowledge of sin." 2- The emotional element: This implies a change of feeling. Sorrow for sin and a desire for pardon are aspects of repentance. (Psalms 51:1) "Have mercy upon me, O God, according to thy lovingkindness: according to the multitude of thy tender mercies blot out my transgressions." 3- The volitional element- This implies a change of will, disposition and purpose. This is the inward turning from sin. There is a change of disposition to seek pardon and cleansing. I remember my youngest son EJ when we went to England. I asked him to carry and watch my professional camera. So, I put the strap around his neck and told him not to remove it from his neck. I jokingly told him that I would rather have him lost than to have my camera lost and EJ look at me like he has a very big question in his mind. And he said, "If I get lost then your camera will get lost too". I said, "That's why you really have to watch…" (Acts 2:38) "Then Peter said unto them, Repent and be baptized everyone of you in the name of Jesus Christ for the remissions of sins, and ye shall receive the gift of the Holy Ghost." The motivation of the heart… It starts from about 18" from the top of your head. Whatever that's in your heart, that's what motivates you to do those things you've done whether for yourself, family or at work place. (Matthew 12:34) "O generation of vipers, how can ye, being evil, speak good things? For out of the abundance of the heart the mouth speaketh." (Matthew 15:19) "For out of the heart proceed evil thoughts, murders, adulteries, fornications, thefts, false witness, blasphemies."

SATURDAY MI DAILY DEVOTION
(I Timothy 1: 4-7)

WORK AT HOME

4- "One that ruleth well his own house, having his children in subjection with all gravity; 5- (For if a man know not how to rule his own house, how shall he take care of the church of God?) 6- Not a novice, lest being lifted up with pride he fall into the condemnation of the devil. 7- Moreover he must have a good report of them which are without; lest he fall into reproach and the snare of the devil."

Here in the United States of America, "work at home" is one of the common words for common people. Who wanted to get up early in the morning, struggle with the traffic and sometimes with the reckless, dangerous, discourteous traffic violators on the road anyways? People would rather stay at home and work at home as much as possible rather than being in the office or workplace. But the question is how do you work at home in terms of taking care of your own home or family? What is the foundation of your home? People would sometimes think that having a beautiful home with fireplace, 2 car garage, beautiful lawn and all the gadgets inside the house will make it a happy and stable home. The foundation of our home must be based on something Heavenly, spiritual and strong.

God must come first. (Matthew 6: 33) "But seek ye first the kingdom of God, and his righteousness; and all these things shall be added unto you."

The Bible must be our guide. (Joshua 1: 8) "This book of the law shall not depart out of thy mouth; but thou shalt meditate therein day and night, that thou mayest observe to do according to all that is written therein: for then thou shalt make thy way prosperous, and then thou shalt have good success." The Word of God should be our guide, our source of knowledge and wisdom. The Word of God should be our map and our path.

I recently attended a seminar about work at home and it was about the internet store which was actually a scheme which was for me could be another "fly by night thing". It was not as I expected it to be. It was a waste of my time and a waste of money. We need faith in the Lord our God and we need the guidance of the Holy Spirit which I believe is very important. We must be conscious of the leading and working of the Holy Spirit of God. Let's ponder on what the writer of the Book of Hebrews says about faith and I know this will really help us in our walk with Him and how we can have it *WORK AT HOME.*

(Hebrews 11: 1-3; 6) 1- "Now faith is the substance of things hoped for, the evidence of things not seen. 2- For by it the elders obtained a good report. 3- Through faith we understand that the worlds were framed by the word of God, so that things which are seen were not made of things which do appear. 6- But without faith it is impossible to please him: for he that cometh to God must believe that he is, and that he is a rewarder of them that diligently seek him."

SUNDAY- MI DAILY DEVOTION
(II Timothy 4:1-8)

CHARGED TIMOTHY

1- "I charge thee therefore before God, and the Lord Jesus Christ, who shall judge the quick and the dead at his appearing and his kingdom; 2- Preach the word; be instant in season, out of season; reprove, rebuke, exhort with all longsuffering and doctrine. 3- For the time will come when they will not endure sound doctrine; but after their own lusts shall they heap to themselves teachers, having itching ears; 4- And they shall turn away their ears from the truth, and shall be turned unto fables. 5- But watch thou in all things, endure afflictions, do the work of an evangelist, make full proof of thy ministry. 6- For I am now ready to be offered, and the time of my departure is at hand. 7- I have fought a good fight, I have finished my course, I have kept the faith: 8- Henceforth there is laid up for me a crown of righteousness, which the Lord, the righteous judge, shall give me at that day: and not to me only, but unto all them also that love his appearing."

Responsibility, accountability and duty are the 3 basic things that could help grow the churches and keep your home and your leadership in a right direction. When Paul said, "I charge thee therefore before God, and the Lord Jesus Christ…" Paul was talking about those 3 basic things, because we are responsible to God as he continues… "… who shall judge the quick and the dead at his appearing and his kingdom; verse 8- "Henceforth there is laid up for me a crown of righteousness, which the Lord, the righteous judge, shall give me at that day: and not to me only, but unto all them also that love his appearing."

Our responsibility is to be ready to preach in good times and in bad times. It is to be ready to share His Words in every seasons of the year. Be it on summer or winter, spring or fall. We are accountable to God for those who are around us, be it a friend, a co- workers or family members, remember that their blood is in our hands. (Ezekiel 3:17- 21) 17- "Son of man, I have made thee a watchman unto the house of Israel: therefore hear the word at my mouth, and give them warning from me. 18- When I say unto the wicked, Thou shalt surely die; and thou givest him not warning, nor speakest to warn the wicked from his wicked way, to save his life; the same wicked man shall die in his iniquity; but his blood will I require at thine hand. 19- Yet if thou warn the wicked, and he turn not from his wickedness, nor from his wicked way, he shall die in his iniquity; but thou hast delivered thy soul. 20- Again,When a righteous man doth turn from his righteousness, and commit iniquity, and I lay a stumblingblock before him, he shall die: because thou hast not given him warning, he shall die in his sin, and his righteousness which he hath done shall not be remembered; but his blood will I require at thine hand. 21- Nevertheless if thou warn the righteous man, that the righteous sin not, and he doth not sin, he shall surely live, because he is warned; also thou hast delivered thy soul." A good and dynamic preacher is not the one who could give you the good definition of term or terms and gives you the Greek and Hebrew meaning or root words of the Scripture verses, but the one who centers his preaching on the Word of God. It's good to have a good and accurate interpretation of the Scriptures and we must, but knowing the definition of terms and root words is not the main thing. The Apostle Paul said that we were sent to preach the gospel. (I Corinthians 1:17- 31) There are 8 important words in verse 18 that you cannot separate from… which are "preaching" "Cross" "them" "perish" "foolishness" "saved" "power" and "God". You cannot separate *preaching* from the *Cross*. Don't take the *Cross* out from your *preaching*. And when you preach about the *Cross* you will always think and talk or preach about *them*; those who will *perish* if they refused to accept the Lord and the free gift of *salvation*. The unbelieving world will *perish* because of their *foolishness*; while those who were *foolish* in the sight of man are those who are *saved* by the *power* of the *Cross* and by the grace of *God*. Verse 21- "For after that in the wisdom of God the world by wisdom knew not God, it pleased God by the foolishness of preaching to save them that believe." Verses 25 to 27 should serve as an encouragement to all of us; 25- "Because the foolishness of God is wiser than men; and the weakness of God is stronger than men. 26- For ye see your calling, brethren, how that not many wise men after the flesh, not many mighty, not many noble, are called: 27- But God hath chosen the foolish things of the world to confound the wise; and God hath chosen the weak things of the world to confound the things which are mighty;"

(Romans 1:21) "Because that, when they knew God, they glorified him not as God, neither were thankful; but became vain in their imaginations, and their foolish heart was darkened."

MONDAY- MI DAILY DEVOTION
(I Thessalonians 1:1-10)

CHRISTIANS ARE LIKE AIRPLANES OR BIRDS?

1- "Paul, and Silvanus, and Timotheus, unto the church of the Thessalonians which is in God the Father and in the Lord Jesus Christ: Grace be unto you, and peace, from God our Father, and the Lord Jesus Christ. 2- We give thanks to God always for you all, making mention of you in our prayers; 3- Remembering without ceasing your work of faith, and labour of love, and patience of hope in our Lord Jesus Christ, in the sight of God and our Father; 4- Knowing, brethren beloved, your election of God. 5- For our gospel came not unto you in word only, but also in power, and in the Holy Ghost, and in much assurance; as ye know what manner of men we were among you for your sake. 6- And ye became followers of us, and of the Lord, having received the word in much affliction, with joy of the Holy Ghost: 7- So that ye were ensamples to all that believe in Macedonia and Achaia. 8- For from you sounded out the word of the Lord not only in Macedonia and Achaia, but also in every place your faith to God-ward is spread abroad; so that we need not to speak anything. 9- For they themselves show of us what manner of entering in we had unto you, and how ye turned to God from idols to serve the living and true God; 10- And to wait for his Son from heaven, whom he raised from the dead, even Jesus, which delivered us from the wrath to come."

The church of the Thessalonians which is in God the Father was a good example of the believers who walks accordingly and according to the Word of God. They have a good testimony of the Lord Jesus Christ. Wherein Paul was not ashamed of... and was not hesitant of lifting them up and giving them the commendation. In verses 2-3- "We give thanks to God always for you all, making mention of you in our prayers; Remembering without ceasing your work of faith, and labour of love, and patience of hope in our Lord Jesus Christ, in the sight of God and our Father;" You may ask a question like, "Why is it that godly Christian life is necessary?" The answer would be in (I Timothy 4:8) 8- "For bodily exercise profiteth little: but godliness is profitable unto all things, having promise of the life that now is, and of that which is to come." It's very clear that godliness as according to Paul is profitable unto all things. Even David himself recognized that living a godly life is of a truth acceptable and well pleasing to God. The Lord will hear our prayers when we live a godly life. Paul was so proud of their faith, of their love, of their patience and hope. I wonder how many churches we have all over the world where Paul could be proud of... and would render the same commendation to such church or churches. Paul was giving thanks to God for the good quality and testimony that they have shown as Christians. The Apostle Paul was praying for them also and for what God was doing in their lives and in their church. They were faithful in performing their duties and executing the Christian faith. Although on Paul's part, it was a prayer of thanksgiving and praise, but it was also a time of recognition and commendation. You can be a crown and joy to your pastor, parents or leader. A crown is something you wear to identify your true identity or something that you wear and to be proud of. (Philippians 4:1) "Therefore, my brethren, dearly beloved and longed for, my joy and crown, so stand fast in the Lord, my dearly beloved."

TUESDAY- MI DAILY DEVOTION
(I Thessalonians 1:1-10)

CHRISTIANS ARE EXAMPLES OF FAITH?

1- "Paul, and Silvanus, and Timotheus, unto the church of the Thessalonians which is in God the Father and in the Lord Jesus Christ: Grace be unto you, and peace, from God our Father, and the Lord Jesus Christ. 2- We give thanks to God always for you all, making mention of you in our prayers; 3- Remembering without ceasing your work of faith, and labour of love, and patience of hope in our Lord Jesus Christ, in the sight of God and our Father; 4- Knowing, brethren beloved, your election of God. 5- For our gospel came not unto you in word only, but also in power, and in the Holy Ghost, and in much assurance; as ye know what manner of men we were among you for your sake. 6- And ye became followers of us, and of the Lord, having received the word in much affliction, with joy of the Holy Ghost: 7- So that ye were ensamples to all that believe in Macedonia and Achaia. 8- For from you sounded out the word of the Lord not only in Macedonia and Achaia, but also in every place your faith to God-ward is spread abroad; so that we need not to speak anything. 9- For they themselves show of us what manner of entering in we had unto you, and how ye turned to God from idols to serve the living and true God; 10- And to wait for his Son from heaven, whom he raised from the dead, even Jesus, which delivered us from the wrath to come."

The church of the Thessalonians as Paul mentioned in verse 1 and the preceding verses "Paul, and Silvanus, and Timotheus, unto the church of the Thessalonians which is in God the Father and in the Lord Jesus Christ…" was a church that follows the leading of Christ and the Holy Spirit and of Paul. Notice verse 6- "And ye became followers of us, and of the Lord, having received the word in much affliction, with joy of the Holy Ghost:"

When you go to some of the grocery stores, they have tables that were set up for their new and old products for people to come and taste or try their samples. It's also their way of letting their consumers know what they have. We are God's examples and God's display of true faith in Him. No wonder Paul said: "So that ye were ensamples to all…" not only to the new believers but to the churches and beyond. Christians should walk the talk and talk the walk. We're like birds or airplanes- we live what we preach. You cannot fly an airplane with just one wing and it's true with the birds. We have to live the Word of God and be an example to our unbelieving love ones, neighbors, co-workers and friends. You cannot just have faith and kept it in your heart. You have to exercise it and live with it and live for it. I understand many of us have heard this phrase which is very true in many sense; "Actions speak louder than words…" It is true with those believers during Paul's time and must be true to you and to this present times believers. Sometimes, when you have a good testimony and you live the Word of God, people will see it and notice it and they will see the difference in you. But you have to stand according to God's Word! (I Thessalonians 1:8) "For from you sounded out the word of the Lord not only in Macedonia and Achaia, but also in every place your faith to God-ward is spread abroad; so that we need not to speak any thing."

WEDNESDAY- MI DAILY DEVOTION
(Psalms 27:1-3)

CONFIDENT IN GOD IN SPITE OF DIFFICULTIES

1- "A Psalm of David. The LORD is my light and my salvation; whom shall I fear? the LORD is the strength of my life; of whom shall I be afraid? 2- When the wicked, even mine enemies and my foes, came upon me to eat up my flesh, they stumbled and fell. 3- Though an host should encamp against me, my heart shall not fear: though war should rise against me, in this will I be confident."

We may not really know the main reasons and the time and the exact location when King David penned this part of Psalms. We may have the general pictures when David wrote this portion of the Scriptures, but one thing for sure; David was facing some difficulties and his only hope and confident was in God. Sometimes the day, time and location will only mean a lot to us after we have overcome. David was facing multitudes of enemies, but fear to David was not a big deal. He learned to trust in God and put his confident in the Almighty. In Verse 3, "Though an host should encamp against me, my heart shall not fear: though war should rise against me, in this will I be confident." That was confident in spite of difficulties and enemies. If the LORD is our Light, our Salvation and our Strength, you can't really ask for more or something else in times of difficulties. In the book of Proverbs 3:25-26 "Be not afraid of sudden fear, neither of the desolation of the wicked, when it cometh. 26- For the LORD shall be thy confidence, and shall keep thy foot from being taken." This time, it's confidence in the midst of sudden fear and desolation.

If you have the SSS- *Salvation, Shepherd and Strength*, your life is complete. Nine years ago, the United States of America went through a lot on 9/11, but in spite of the difficulties we went through, we have confidence in God and we made it. (Psalm 27:5- 14) 5- "For in the time of trouble he shall hide me in his pavilion: in the secret of his tabernacle shall he hide me; he shall set me up upon a rock. 6- And now shall mine head be lifted up above mine enemies round about me: therefore will I offer in his tabernacle sacrifices of joy; I will sing, yea, I will sing praises unto the LORD. 7- Hear, O LORD, when I cry with my voice: have mercy also upon me, and answer me. 8- When thou saidst, Seek ye my face; my heart said unto thee, Thy face, LORD, will I seek. 9- Hide not thy face far from me; put not thy servant away in anger: thou hast been my help; leave me not, neither forsake me, O God of my salvation. 10- When my father and my mother forsake me, then the LORD will take me up. 11- Teach me thy way, O LORD, and lead me in a plain path, because of mine enemies. 12- Deliver me not over unto the will of mine enemies: for false witnesses are risen up against me, and such as breathe out cruelty. 13- I had fainted, unless I had believed to see the goodness of the LORD in the land of the living. 14- Wait on the LORD: be of good courage, and he shall strengthen thine heart: wait, I say, on the LORD."

THURSDAY- MI DAILY DEVOTION
(Proverbs 4:1-8)

DAD, ARE YOU OK?

1- "Hear, ye children, the instruction of a father, and attend to know understanding. 2- For I give you good doctrine, forsake ye not my law. 3- For I was my father's son, tender and only beloved in the sight of my mother. 4- He taught me also, and said unto me, Let thine heart retain my words: keep my commandments, and live. 5- Get wisdom, get understanding: forget it not; neither decline from the words of my mouth. 6- Forsake her not, and she shall preserve thee: love her, and she shall keep thee. 7- Wisdom is the principal thing; therefore get wisdom: and with all thy getting get understanding. 8- Exalt her, and she shall promote thee: she shall bring thee to honour, when thou dost embrace her."

I preached this message on Father's Day and let me share this to you. Are we OK...? NO, we're not OK if... we're making bad decisions... if we are not doing our duties right and in a godly way and if we don't have a dream... a dream that will make a difference. Have a dream that could turn your world, your church and your home upside down.

HAPPY FATHER'S DAY!!! To the dad's out there... DECISIONS, DECISIONS, DECISIONS... Your decisions as a father will determine the future of your children and your home. We need to have a right, good and godly decision making. Commit everything to God and don't make any *MAJOR* decisions when you're angry, spiritually down or depress. You might be the only guide and footsteps your children will follow. Pray and pray hard for your relationship with your wife, your children and your church as well as the decisions you make. God will bless you for that and keep it up.

DUTY, DUTY AND DUTIES... yes being a father it means a duty and more duties. Be faithful to your *DUTIES* as a father. You are responsible to God for undone duties and any duties that you have done halfheartedly. You may call it the way you want to call it, but the bottom line is... you have duties as a father, responsibilities and accountability to your family and to God.

DREAM, DREAM AND DREAM... YES DREAM SOMETHING BIG FOR YOUR FAMILY. You are where you are by how you look at life from the inside out. It must start from your heart and mind. If you're happy with what you have and what you are in all areas of your life right now and you're not stepping up on the next level, because of lack of dream; then you will be the same person, the same DAD that people will see including your children few years back and in the future. (Proverbs 23:7) "For as he thinketh in his heart, so is he: Eat and drink, saith he to thee; but his heart is not with thee." Let us be like Habakkuk, check out what he said in the Book of Habakkuk. (Habakkuk 1: 1- 2) 1- "I will stand upon my watch, and set me upon the tower, and will watch to see what he will say unto me, and what I shall answer when I am reproved. 2- And the LORD answered me, and said, Write the vision, and make it plain upon tables, that he may run that readeth it. 3- For the vision is yet for an appointed time, but at the end it shall speak, and not lie: though it tarry, wait for it; because it will surely come, it will not tarry."

FRIDAY- MI DAILY DEVOTION
(Matthew 6:6-8)

THE OLDEST PHONE LINE OR CELL PHONE- *PRAYER*

6- "But thou, when thou prayest, enter into thy closet, and when thou hast shut thy door, pray to thy Father which is in secret; and thy Father which seeth in secret shall reward thee openly. 7-But when ye pray, use not vain repetitions, as the heathen do: for they think that they shall be heard for their much speaking. 8- Be not ye therefore like unto them: for your Father knoweth what things ye have need of, before ye ask him."

John Bunyan once said, "Prayer will make a man cease from sin, or sin will entice a man to cease from prayer." As you humble yourself and as you're on your knees to God in the spirit of prayer, you are using your phone line to heaven free of charge... plus the benefit of its answers and blessings. Sin in our lives can cause a complete breakdown of our communication or cell phone to heaven which is your prayer life. (Psalms 66:18) "If I regard iniquity in my heart, the Lord will not hear me:"

(Isaiah 59:1-2) 1- "Behold, the LORD'S hand is not shortened, that it cannot save; neither his ear heavy, that it cannot hear: 2- But your iniquities have separated between you and your God, and your sins have hid his face from you, that he will not hear."

I believe that some of the Christians are sincere, serious and really love to pray, but they have so much unanswered prayers because of sin. I believe, as it is written in the Scriptures that the answer is just a prayer away. The throne of God is open as you humbly confess your sins and ask the Lord to forgive you as you lay down your needs, your problems and may be your complaints to God (although it sounds negative) but it could be true to many Christians.

(I Peter 5:6-7) "Humble yourselves therefore under the mighty hand of God, that he may exalt you in due time: 7- Casting all your care upon him; for he careth for you."

"Beginning the day with a devotional Bible study and prayer equips a man for the day's fight with self and sin and Satan."- (John R Mott) The Lord Jesus Christ has His own quiet time with the Father; when He went into a desert place to be alone with the Father and when He was in the garden of Gethsemane as the Father ushered Him to Calvary to be crucified for our sins and salvation. When Joseph was in the process of God's molding and preparations, God put him in the pit so Joseph could be alone with God. God was preparing Joseph for a greater responsibilities and blessings. It was from being a delivery boy for his brethren to a greater deliverance for a fallen nation. (Genesis 37: 23-24).

God is honored when you are on your knees for prayer and confession. Just humble yourself under the mighty hand of God and God will take care of business. God will help you with all kinds of God honoring and God glorifying business. You just have to ask or pray to God. Prayer and the Word of God are inseparable… It's almost impossible to read your Bible and not pray or to pray and not read your Bible. (Proverbs 28:9) "He that turneth away his ear from hearing the law, even his prayer shall be abomination."

SATURDAY- MI DAILY DEVOTION
(Matthew 6:9-13)

PRAY- *"LORD, THY WILL BE DONE…"*

9- "After this manner therefore pray ye: Our Father which art in heaven, Hallowed be thy name. 10- Thy kingdom come. Thy will be done in earth, as it is in heaven. 11- Give us this day our daily bread. 12- And forgive us our debts, as we forgive our debtors. 13- And lead us not into temptation, but deliver us from evil: For thine is the kingdom, and the power, and the glory, for ever. Amen."

I remember a man who was standing before his wife's deathbed and later knelt down to pray for her healing. And after a little while, he prayed- "Lord, not my will, but thine be done…"

The Lord Jesus Christ when He was here on earth taught His disciples how *not* to live in the flesh. As Christians, we have been taught by the Holy Spirit to live in the Spirit and not in the flesh. Even in our prayers, God wants for us to pray according to His will. Prayer is really a big thing for many religious groups, but prayer is the Christian's opportunity, responsibility and life. (Proverbs 15:8) "The sacrifice of the wicked is an abomination to the LORD: but the prayer of the upright is his delight." It is God's will for us Christians to pray and to pray in His will. When you pray to God, "Lord, Thy will be done," it means that in humility and full obedience, you are really willing to submit your will to His will and your want to what God wants for you. You let God do what's best for you. We have no will of our own as God's servants but only His will. It shows the recognition of our frailty and of our love for the one who gave His life for us and for the salvation of our souls. We always want the best for ourselves and we always desire the best in answer to our prayers. Everyone desires the best for themselves and for their family. There's nothing better than God's will in our lives and there's nothing better than what God has in stored for us. I like this beautiful hymn about prayer. *In The Garden*

I come to the garden alone
While the dew is still on the roses
And the voice I hear falling on my ear
The Son of God discloses.

And He walks with me, and He talks with me,
And He tells me I am His own;
And the joy we share as we tarry there,
None other has ever known.

He speaks, and the sound of His voice,
Is so sweet the birds hush their singing,
And the melody that He gave to me
Within my heart is ringing…
(Charles Austin Miles- 1912)

His *will* not my *will*, and notice what John said in the Book of (John 15:7) "If ye abide in me, and my words abide in you, ye shall ask what ye will, and it shall be done unto you."

(I John 5: 14- 15) "And this is the confidence that we have in him, that, if we ask any thing according to his will, he heareth us: 15- And if we know that he hear us, whatsoever we ask, we know that we have the petitions that we desired of him."

(Jeremiah 29:11-13) 11- "For I know the thoughts that I think toward you, saith the LORD, thoughts of peace, and not of evil, to give you an expected end. 12- Then shall ye call upon me, and ye shall go and pray unto me, and I will hearken unto you. 13- And ye shall seek me, and find me, when ye shall search for me with all your heart."

SUNDAY- MI DAILY DEVOTION
(Matthew 7:7-11)

THE SEVEN ELEVEN PRINCIPLES

7- "Ask, and it shall be given you; seek, and ye shall find; knock, and it shall be opened unto you: 8- For every one that asketh receiveth; and he that seeketh findeth; and to him that knocketh it shall be opened. 9- Or what man is there of you, whom if his son ask bread, will he give him a stone? 10- Or if he ask a fish, will he give him a serpent? 11- If ye then, being evil, know how to give good gifts unto your children, how much more shall your Father which is in heaven give good things to them that ask him?"

This portion is not sponsored by 7-Eleven retail stores. This is the Lord's principles about prayer as mentioned in Matthew chapter 7 verses 7 to 11. I assumed you got my point why the title of this portion of MI DAILY DEVOTION is THE SEVEN ELEVEN PRINCIPLES.

You may dream something big and desire something that someone never dreamed of. It might be the best thing for you and it may look like it's the best. But the question is- is it the will of God for you? We really have to think, plan, and consult God first before taking a move or a step forward even in our prayer. Some of the questions that we may personally ask ourselves before asking God for His approval or answer would be:

1. Will this be God honoring and God glorifying?
2. Will this be edifying to the body of Christ which is the church?

3. Will this help me grow in grace and in the knowledge of the Lord Jesus Christ?
4. Could this help me be a better Christian or person?
5. Is this a selfish desire or a self- *less* desire?
6. Is this the right time?
7. If God answers my prayer, what's next?

Will this be beneficial to God's purpose, my future plans, my family and my church? Submitting to God's will even in our prayer life will always make the difference. We should never be afraid to ask God for anything if it is His will. (Matthew 7:7-8) "Ask, and it shall be given you; seek, and ye shall find; knock, and it shall be opened unto you: 8- For every one that asketh receiveth; and he that seeketh findeth; and to him that knocketh it shall be opened."

I believe as what the Lord said in those verses that we should not only ask but seek and seek His will with determination and humility. (I Peter 5: 5-6) "Likewise, ye younger, submit yourselves unto the elder. Yea, all of you be subject one to another, and be clothed with humility: for God resisteth the proud, and giveth grace to the humble. 6- Humble yourselves therefore under the mighty hand of God, that he may exalt you in due time:" (I John 5:14-15) 14- "And this is the confidence that we have in him, that, if we ask anything according to his will, he heareth us: 15- And if we know that he hear us, whatsoever we ask, we know that we have the petitions that we desired of him." What a promise we have there from the Books of Matthew and I John. So Christians, if you think and you know and you have the assurance and the confirmation that what you're praying for is God's will for you, then pray for it and be determined to GO for it. In my personal experiences as a Christian, if there's something that God has placed in my heart, be it a ministry related desire or dreams, a personal or family related desire and dreams, I will not stop desiring and praying for such until God will take it away from my heart. I have countless of desires and dreams that I asked the Lord for… I know God had placed in my heart and I kept them in my heart and prayed for them until I got the answers. One of the big dreams was seeking His will the day I met Vem, who is now my life partner. I remember the day when we planned of settling down for the future as we prepared for a simple wedding. Back then, I was just a new Christian and I was on my first year in the Bible College or Seminary. It was the very first time in my life where I was really serious about relationship and was seeking God's hand upon our marriage. Seeking God's will is not that easy. It's a spiritual battle because the devil will stop you and hinder you and will destroy you, your plans and desires for God and your family. But let me just encourage you. Keep it up and be determined and keep praying and dreaming for greater blessings.

(Matthew 26: 38-39) "Then saith he unto them, My soul is exceeding sorrowful, even unto death: tarry ye here, and watch with me. 39- And he went a little farther, and fell on his face, and prayed, saying, O my Father, if it be possible, let this cup pass from me: nevertheless not as I will, but as thou wilt."

MONDAY- MI DAILY DEVOTION
(I Peter 4:12-16)

WHY SUFFERING IS THE LORD'S BLESSING TO CHRISTIANS?

12- "Beloved, think it not strange concerning the fiery trial which is to try you, as though some strange thing happened unto you: 13- But rejoice, inasmuch as ye are partakers of Christ's sufferings; that, when his glory shall be revealed, ye may be glad also with exceeding joy. 14- If ye be reproached for the name of Christ, happy are ye; for the spirit of glory and of God resteth upon you: on their part he is evil spoken of, but on your part he is glorified. 15- But let none of you suffer as a murderer, or as a thief, or as an evildoer, or as a busybody in other men's matters. 16- Yet if any man suffer as a Christian, let him not be ashamed; but let him glorify God on this behalf."

I used to pastor a small church in Makati, Manila in the Philippines. I have a church member who was going through sufferings. We all know that Christians don't always call it problem, but trials, tribulation or suffering. Anyways, I told him that it seems that you are going through tough times and looks like your suffering was just too much for you and your family. And I was surprised when he said: "My suffering is a blessing in disguise and I know it pastor…" It would be hard to say that, unless you live the faith and you're living by the faith of the Son of God. Yes, if you're a Christian and you are living by faith, you will see God's hand in your trials and sufferings. A believer who have experienced the grace of God in his/her suffering can always looked back and see God's interventions and miracle in his/

her suffering. (Job 23:10) "But he knoweth the way that I take: when he hath tried me, I shall come forth as gold." Suffering produces good character, patient and humility. There's an easy way out, but there will be no rewards. There will be some easy way out, but God's hand and blessings will not be there. There's a one way exit, but you will be on your road to point of no return. You can step out of God given suffering and miss the results of God's reward or blessings. I exactly know what it means to suffer. People who are close to me and know me, knows what I've been through and have witnessed the pain that I've gone through. Be it personal, physical, financial, church or ministry related suffering. I remember growing up in a very poor family where life was just so tough. Sometimes, my parents can't even afford to buy sugar for our coffee. We oftentimes have porridge on our table with no sugar or salt on it. We would usually go to school without any breakfast but coffee. I would sometimes come home with stomach pain for hunger and starvation. I assumed you get the picture of hardship that I went through when I was growing up. But you don't quit in the midst of suffering, because you are in God's processing aisle where only God knows what's best for you and what you are going through. God knows where you will end up during the process and just like what Job said: "When he hath tried me, I shall come forth as gold." Keep this in your heart and mind. Be reminded of this that an easy way out is not a blessing and that God is not done with you yet. You are still in the processing plant of God. He wants to see a good, excellent finished product out of you which is your character. God will be honored and glorified in you and through you. (Ephesians 2:10) "For we are his workmanship, created in Christ Jesus unto good works, which God hath before ordained that we should walk in them." (Romans 8:17-18) 17- "And if children, then heirs; heirs of God, and joint-heirs with Christ; if so be that we suffer with him, that we may be also glorified together. 18- For I reckon that the sufferings of this present time are not worthy to be compared with the glory which shall be revealed in us."

TUESDAY MI DAILY DEVOTION
(I Peter 4:1; 12-16)

STAY IN THE RING!!!

1- "Forasmuch then as Christ hath suffered for us in the flesh, arm yourselves likewise with the same mind: for he that hath suffered in the flesh hath ceased from sin;" 12- "Beloved, think it not strange concerning the fiery trial which is to try you, as though some strange thing happened unto you: 13- But rejoice, inasmuch as ye are partakers of Christ's sufferings; that, when his glory shall be revealed, ye may be glad also with exceeding joy. 14- If ye be reproached for the name of Christ, happy are ye; for the spirit of glory and of God resteth upon you: on their part he is evil spoken of, but on your part he is glorified. 15- But let none of you suffer as a murderer, or as a thief, or as an evildoer, or as a busybody in other men's matters. 16- Yet if any man suffer as a Christian, let him not be ashamed; but let him glorify God on this behalf."

It's not because Christ has suffered in the flesh, so must we. But as believers, we must condition our heart and mind that suffering is a part of Christian life and even life itself. Someone said that as a disciple of the Lord Jesus Christ, we were given the privilege to wear 3 rings: which are *engagement ring*, *wedding ring* and *suffer-ring*. I believe that many of us wear at least one of those rings. But let me give you another ring which is very important and needful as you proudly wear those *rings*. You need to *STAY IN THE RING*. It's good to be engaged and it's even great to be married and proudly wear that wedding ring that you have, but as you enter in, in the arena of a married life, your life will never be the same again. It would not be like the movie you've watched on your wide screen that the Hollywood have had produced for our own pleasure or entertainment. We are in a real life drama and action. Don't throw the towel off from the *"ring of life"* or don't throw that wedding ring off your arena. You have to keep your eyes on Jesus who suffered for us and for our sins. You may think that *suffer- ring* is the kind of *ring* that will not really excite you like the 2 previous *rings*. But don't be afraid of suffering. Yes, it may sound funny, but it's true. Being engaged or being married would only meant love, joy, happiness, blessings, kids and so much more… But it comes with suffering, problems and trials. It means you have to be ready for that. It's the same way with our Christian life. Your life will never be the same when you humbly come to God in the name of the Lord Jesus Christ, when you ask Him to come into your life. The day you accept the Lord as your Lord and Savior and ask Him to forgive you of your sins… God has given you the authority to become His Child. (John 1:12) "But as many as received him, to them gave he power to become the sons of God, even to them that believe on his name:" You are now a saved person or a disciple of Christ. It means you are Christ's follower and you are His church. Christ has given us His life as a sacrifice. (Ephesians 5:2) "And walk in love, as Christ also hath loved us, and hath given himself for us an offering and a sacrifice to God for a sweetsmelling savour." Now, as a disciple of the Lord Jesus Christ, you will have suffering, even if you're living a holy, consecrated and a devoted life for God. (I Peter 4:12-13) Trials and suffering should not be a big surprise to us from God. Verse 12- "Beloved, think it not strange concerning the fiery trial which is to try you …" Verse 13- "But rejoice, inasmuch as ye are partakers of Christ's sufferings;" We know that it will not be easy, but Apostle Paul said: "But rejoice…" Why? Because we are partakers of Christ's suffering. It means that it is a privilege and an honor to be partakers of His suffering. So you better be in that *ring* and *stay in the ring,* where God is working in you and through you.

(II Timothy 4:5-7) "But watch thou in all things, endure afflictions, do the work of an evangelist, make full proof of thy ministry. 6- For I am now ready to be offered, and the time of my departure is at hand. 7- I have fought a good fight, I have finished my course, I have kept the faith:"

WEDNESDAY- MI DAILY DEVOTION
(Job 23:14)

"FOR HE PERFORMETH THE THINGS THAT HE APPOINTED FOR ME:"

"10- But he knoweth the way that I take: when he hath tried me, I shall come forth as gold. 11- My foot hath held his steps, his way have I kept, and not declined. 12- Neither have I gone back from the commandment of his lips; I have esteemed the words of his mouth more than my necessary food. 13- But he is in one mind, and who can turn him? and what his soul desireth, even that he doeth. 14- For he performeth the thing that is appointed for me: and many such things are with him. 15- Therefore am I troubled at his presence: when I consider, I am afraid of him. 16- For God maketh my heart soft, and the Almighty troubleth me: 17- Because I was not cut off before the darkness, neither hath he covered the darkness from my face."

We are walking in the path God has prepared for us. We are doing the things God has appointed for us. God never waste His time performing the things that He has appointed for every human being living in this world. God has His own purposes, desires and plans for every human being in which we have messed them up real bad. But in spite of what we've done with our lives and what we've done with God's plan for the ages, we can still look up to Him and trust God in His *Purpose*… (Romans 8:28) "And we know that all things work together for good to them that love God, to them who are the called according to his purpose." Although we really displeased God in so many ways, in spite of that, we can always rely on Him especially in His great love for us. I can't remember who, when and where, but the only thing that I know and remember was the quotation of this preacher. He said: "Every wind that blows can only fill your sails." Not only that we can trust in the purpose of God in our lives, but we can also trust in His *power*… (Jeremiah 51:15) "He hath made the earth by his power, he hath established the world by his wisdom, and hath stretched out the heaven and the heaven of heavens by his understanding." Let me call this verse the "3 H's" - which means that God did all those by the power of His *hand*, from His *heart* as demonstrated in His love for us. Everything was created by God and was done based on His unfathomed intellect. The Lord in His great mind and intellect prepared to us the blessings and the future. Jesus is the *head* of the church of the living God and He knows what's ahead of us. (I Chronicles 29:11) "Thine, O LORD, is the greatness, and the power, and the glory, and the victory, and the majesty: for all that is in the heaven and in the earth is thine; thine is the kingdom, O LORD, and thou art exalted as head above all." God has all the power to give and provides. And He has all the power to fight for you and to fight your battle of any sorts. And one of the good thing and very encouraging thing is… we can Trust in the *Promises* of God. God did not promise us that He will give us everything, but God has promised us something and we can lean on Him for His great blessings. We can also trust Him for every promise that we have from the Scriptures as recorded in (Proverbs 3:5-6) "Trust in the LORD with all thine heart; and lean not unto thine own understanding. 6- In all thy ways acknowledge him, and he shall direct thy paths."

THURSDAY- MI DAILY DEVOTION
(Job 23:10- 17)

"TRUST HIS HEART"

10- "But he knoweth the way that I take: when he hath tried me, I shall come forth as gold. 11- My foot hath held his steps, his way have I kept, and not declined. 12- Neither have I gone back from the commandment of his lips; I have esteemed the words of his mouth more than my necessary food. 13- But he is in one mind, and who can turn him? and what his soul desireth, even that he doeth. 14- For he performeth the thing that is appointed for me: and many such things are with him. 15- Therefore am I troubled at his presence: when I consider, I am afraid of him. 16- For God maketh my heart soft, and the Almighty troubleth me: 17- Because I was not cut off before the darkness, neither hath he covered the darkness from my face."

So you have tried your best, did it your way, work hard and did things in the flesh and the conclusion was; it did not work? Have you asked God for His direction or seek God's wisdom? That was the questions I asked a young man who was seeking my advice or counsel. Whatever God is doing in our lives, He is doing it with a purpose and with a *Plan*. Christians we ought to trust His *plan*. I heard a preacher say this which could be true to you, he said: "Everything we have to do... and everything we have to bear..., all comes to us as part of His pre-arranged plan." There was a song which says; "Trust His Heart..." I love what Apostle Paul said in the Book of Romans and please read the whole chapter really slow and meditate on it. (Romans 8:24- 28) 24- "For we are saved by hope: but hope that is seen is not hope: for what a man seeth, why doth he yet hope for? 25- But if we hope for that we see not, then do we with patience wait for it. 26- Likewise the Spirit also helpeth our infirmities: for we know not what we should pray for as we ought: but the Spirit itself maketh intercession for us with groanings which cannot be uttered. 27- And he that searcheth the hearts knoweth what is the mind of the Spirit, because he maketh intercession for the saints according to the will of God. 28- And we know that all things work together for good to them that love God, to them who are the called according to his purpose." I don't really know how many of our readers could identify with this phrase, "God is too wise to be mistaken and God is too good to be unkind…"

No one knows what will happen next… If you recall the 911 that killed thousands of innocent people. We did not know and what was the plan of God when the Katrina tragedy happened in 2005. Only God knows why He let things happens to individual, homes and nations. (Psalm 37: 18; 23- 24) "The LORD knoweth the days of the upright: and their inheritance shall be forever. 23- The steps of a good man are ordered by the LORD: and he delighteth in his way. 24- Though he fall, he shall not be utterly cast down: for the LORD upholdeth him with his hand." All we have to do is to trust in Him and trust His heart. Do you still remember the earthquake and the tsunami in 2004 that kills thousands of people in an instant? Although, we all know that the end is near and the Lord's coming is closer than we think, but the best thing to know is… God is in control and we must learn to trust Him. (Psalms 32: 10) "Many sorrows shall be to the wicked: but he that trusteth in the LORD, mercy shall compass him about." (Psalm 37: 3) 3- "Trust in the LORD, and do good; so shalt thou dwell in the land, and verily thou shalt be fed."

FRIDAY- MI DAILY DEVOTION
(Philippians 4:16- 20)

GOD'S PROVISION AND GRACE

16- "For even in Thessalonica ye sent once and again unto my necessity. 17- Not because I desire a gift: but I desire fruit that may abound to your account. 18- But I have all, and abound: I am full, having received of Epaphroditus the things which were sent from you, an odour of a sweet smell, a sacrifice acceptable, wellpleasing to God. 19- But my God shall supply all your need according to his riches in glory by Christ Jesus. 20- Now unto God and our Father be glory for ever and ever. Amen."

Do you have something for your son when he comes home…? That was actually the question of my mother to my dad when they were still alive. It was about my brother who at the time was in a seminary in Bacolod City, Philippines. It was a beautiful Sunday morning when my mom woke up with that question for my dad. My mom was asking him if he has money or something like food and goodies for my younger brother when he comes home for the weekend. And my dad said: "No" with that being said, my dad decided not to go to church. My dad's reasons were to save the money they intended to use for public transportation as well as their tithes and offering. But my mom as she relates the story to me said: "It doesn't matter if we have food on the table or nothing for him, when Ephraim comes home from his church today, we will be in our church and we will just pray for the needs here while at church." And to make the long story short, when they all came home from church… there was food and goodies on the table and the money was provided. Until the day my parents went to be with the Lord, they did not have any idea where those food and goodies came from. She did not give me the detail about the money. I don't know why Christians knows that God is the creator and giver of this life. We know that God loves us and He gave us His only begotten Son to die for us. We know that He can work miraculously and He is the *provider*, but the question is: "Do we put our trust in Him that He will provide our needs.

Abraham was busy preparing his son Isaac and the altar where he will offer him to God as God has required of him. This is a very beautiful story of God's timely provision. Check out on how God provided the sacrifice. The Lord gave him his son's (Isaac) back and the Lord also provided the offering as they worship. (Genesis 22:2-6) 2- "And he said, Take now thy son, thine only son Isaac, whom thou lovest, and get thee into the land of Moriah; and offer him there for a burnt offering upon one of the mountains which I will tell thee of. 3- And Abraham rose up early in the morning, and saddled his ass, and took two of his young men with him, and Isaac his son, and clave the wood for the burnt offering, and rose up, and went unto the place of which God had told him. 4- Then on the third day Abraham lifted up his eyes, and saw the place afar off. 5- And Abraham said unto his young men, Abide ye here with the ass; and I and the lad will go yonder and worship, and come again to you. 6- And Abraham took the wood of the burnt offering, and laid it upon Isaac his son; and he took the fire in his hand, and a knife; and they went both of them together."

SATURDAY- MI DAILY DEVOTION
(Colossians 3:15-16)

OUR JOY OF WORSHIP COMES WITH SALVATION, PRAYER AND PRAISE.

15- "And let the peace of God rule in your hearts, to the which also ye are called in one body; and be ye thankful. 16- Let the word of Christ dwell in you richly in all wisdom; teaching and admonishing one another in psalms and hymns and spiritual songs, singing with grace in your hearts to the Lord."

An individual has to know Him first as Savior and Lord before you can really worship Him in Spirit and in truth. (John 4:23-23- "But the hour cometh, and now is, when the true worshippers shall worship the Father in spirit and in truth: for the Father seeketh such to worship him. 24- God is a Spirit: and they that worship him must worship him in spirit and in truth."

How can you personally know that you truly and personally know Him as your Lord and Savior? One of the many questions I've encountered while witnessing was: "Why do I need to accept Christ as my Lord and Savior when I already accepted Him since I was a little child and when I had my first communion?" And one of their issues is: "I have and I do accept Christ in my mind, always…" But to accept the Lord Jesus Christ in your heart means to put your trust in Him and Him alone and let Him come into your empty soul. You let Him control your whole being. You let Him be the Lord of your life. (John 1:12) "But as many as received him, to them gave he power to become the sons of God, even to them that believe on his name:" Believe in Him as your

Savior and that He alone can save you by His death on the Cross, His burial and resurrection. People would sometime argue with me and would say: "We always believe in God and we know that there is a God that exists". This could be partly true, because believing or faith has different meaning to different people or religion. You have to confess your sins to Him. (I John 1:8-9) 8- "If we say that we have no sin, we deceive ourselves, and the truth is not in us." 9- If we confess our sins, he is faithful and just to forgive us our sins, and to cleanse us from all unrighteousness." People sometimes misunderstand the true meaning of confession in the Bible. But here is Paul's idea of confession as according to God's view; "So then faith cometh by hearing, and hearing by the word of God." God has to capture your heart and mind. (Romans 10:8- 13; 17) 8- "But what saith it? The word is nigh thee, even in thy mouth, and in thy heart: that is, the word of faith, which we preach; 9- That if thou shalt confess with thy mouth the Lord Jesus, and shalt believe in thine heart that God hath raised him from the dead, thou shalt be saved. 10- For with the heart man believeth unto righteousness; and with the mouth confession is made unto salvation. 11- For the scripture saith, Whosoever believeth on him shall not be ashamed. 12- For there is no difference between the Jew and the Greek: for the same Lord over all is rich unto all that call upon him. 13; 17- For whosoever shall call upon the name of the Lord shall be saved." Once you have Christ in your heart, then true worship, praise and prayer will follow. The joy of worship comes along with fellowship by prayer and praise.

SUNDAY- MI DAILY DEVOTION
(Philippians 4:5- 7)

GOD'S WAY TO GO UP IS TO GO DOWN

5- "Let your moderation be known unto all men. The Lord is at hand. 6- Be careful for nothing; but in every thing by prayer and supplication with thanksgiving let your requests be made known unto God. 7- And the peace of God, which passeth all understanding, shall keep your hearts and minds through Christ Jesus."

This peace will *keep our hearts and minds through Christ Jesus;* it will keep us from sinning under our troubles and from sinking under them; keep us calm and sedated, without discomposure of passion, with inward satisfaction. *Thou wilt keep him in perfect peace whose mind is stayed on thee,* (Isaiah 26:3). Matthew Henry

"It is easy to focus on your devotions rather than the object of your devotions. Do your best to focus on God rather than the discipline of daily devotions." The reason why God wants us to devote ourselves to prayer is because he wants you to know that He listens. When you pray earnestly, God promises to answer in ways that will amaze you. Much of what happens in my life and your life as well whether insignificant or catastrophic was really beyond our control. I did not have any control at the death of my parents and 2 brothers whom I love and really dear to my heart. But I thank God, He is in control. We must thank the Lord for everything in our prayers. Prayer must express Adoration, Confession, Thanksgiving and Supplication. (ACTS)

Someone writes: "We can give thanks in everything and say 'Thy will be done,' for God's at work in everything to make us like His Son." The only way for us to *GO UP* is to *GO DOWN* on our knees. If you can't sleep at night, don't count sheep, count on the Shepherd.

As for me, the best way to be humbled by the Lord is when he brings me down to my knees. In order for us to rise up, we must first get down and humble ourselves in prayer. The more we keep our hearts and minds through Christ Jesus, the more God becomes closer to us. He will pick us up and draw us closer to Him. (Isaiah 26:3) "Thou wilt keep him in perfect peace, whose mind is stayed on thee: because he trusteth in thee." When God took Jeremiah to a Potter's house so he could be alone with Him, he was being prepared of the Lord like clay in the hands of the Potter. God caused him to go through the breaking for a great revival and repentance of the nation (Jeremiah 18). The Lord Jesus Christ has His own quiet time with the Father when He went into a desert place to be alone with the Father and when He was in the Garden of Gethsemane as the Father ushered Him to Calvary to be crucified for our sins and salvation. Try the formula of Peter for all of us of which I know and believe that it really works. (I Peter 5:5-7) "Likewise, ye younger, submit yourselves unto the elder. Yea, all of you be subject one to another, and be clothed with humility: for God resisteth the proud, and giveth grace to the humble. 6- Humble yourselves therefore under the mighty hand of God, that he may exalt you in due time: 7- Casting all your care upon him; for he careth for you."

MONDAY- MI DAILY DEVOTION
(Proverbs 23:7)

THE DEVIL'S DEVICES

"For as he thinketh in his heart, so is he: Eat and drink, saith he to thee; but his heart is not with thee."

"If you think you can, you can. If you think you are, you are." John Maxwell.

What is the best part of your life? What is the most significant moment in the history of your life? You may know your biography and geography, but without knowing your theology and your Creator, your life history would be meaningless.

The devil has a deceptive plan to every human being. He offers the world everything it wants and desires only to lead it to its own destruction. Remember the temptation of Jesus? Here in the Book of Matthew, the devil knew that Jesus was weak physically due to the Lord's 40 days of fasting and prayer. Satan took the opportunity to seduced Jesus and offered Him all the worldly pleasures. He also offered the Lord Jesus Christ power and protection. (Matthew 4:1-11) 1- "Then was Jesus led up of the Spirit into the wilderness to be tempted of the devil. 2- And when he had fasted forty days and forty nights, he was afterward an hungered. 3- And when the tempter came to him, he said, If thou be the Son of God, command that these stones be made bread. 4- But he answered and said, It is written, Man shall not live by bread alone, but by every word that proceedeth out of the mouth of God. 5- Then the devil taketh him up into the holy city, and setteth him on a pinnacle of the temple, 6- And saith unto him, If thou be the Son of God, cast thyself down: for it is written, He shall give his angels charge concerning thee: and in their hands they shall bear thee up, lest at any time thou dash thy foot against a stone. 7- Jesus said unto him, It is written again, Thou shalt not tempt the Lord thy God. 8- Again, the devil taketh him up into an exceeding high mountain, and showeth him all the kingdoms of the world, and the glory of them; 9- And saith unto him, All these things will I give thee, if thou wilt fall down and worship me. 10- Then saith Jesus unto him, Get thee hence, Satan: for it is written, Thou shalt worship the Lord thy God, and him only shalt thou serve. 11- Then the devil leaveth him, and, behold, angels came and ministered unto him." You can't really win over Satan's devices and deception but by the power of the Word of God and by the Blood of the Lamb… we have the victory. Jesus Himself used the Word of God to resists and rebuked Satan and his temptation and deception. (Ephesians 6: 17) "And take the helmet of salvation, and the sword of the Spirit, which is the word of God:" The devil has something more to offer to us in a minute than what God will give us in 10 years, but the outcome or the results will be different. The devil can do the same to you as what he tried to do to Jesus, but miserably failed. It's so easy for him to promise us something and do different things. He is a deceiver even from the beginning. (John 8: 44) "Ye are of your father the devil, and the lusts of your father ye will do. He was a murderer from the beginning, and abode not in the truth, because there is no truth in him. When he speaketh a lie, he speaketh of his own: for he is a liar, and the father of it." Temptation comes from the devil. Be watchful, sober and vigilant. Satan was likened into a lion who hunts an animal to devour.

The enemy is seeking for someone to tempt and destroy. Let us be reminded of the devil's operations, tactics and devices. Peter warned us about the adversary which is the devil. (I Peter 5:8) "Be sober, be vigilant; because your adversary the devil, as a roaring lion, walketh about, seeking whom he may devour:"

TUESDAY- MI DAILY DEVOTION
(Genesis 2:15-17)

THE DEVIL- DESTROYER, DECEPTIVE AND DIRTY

15- "And the LORD God took the man, and put him into the garden of Eden to dress it and to keep it. 16- And the LORD God commanded the man, saying, Of every tree of the garden thou mayest freely eat: 17- But of the tree of the knowledge of good and evil, thou shalt not eat of it: for in the day that thou eatest thereof thou shalt surely die."

The devil will feed you according to his disposal, will and selfish desires. He wants to sip you like wheat. As much as God has His banquet table for His children, the devil has his own too. The difference is that God satisfies and blesses His children. The enemy will feed you and satisfy you temporarily so he can execute his destructive plans.

Proverbs 23:7) "For as he thinketh in his heart, so is he: Eat and drink, saith he to thee; but his heart is not with thee."

I believe that that's the same words that the enemy will tell us. "Eat and drink…" The devil and his angels wanted to duplicate what God is doing and as Who God is and how He works in the lives of His children. It is very obvious that he imitates what God is doing to His creation and most especially to His children. I have seen so many lives, so many ministers and minister's wives as well as churches that were destroyed by the devil. I've seen families, businesses and children that were destroyed by the enemy. It breaks my heart how I've watched these pastors built their church or ministries and just to be scrambled in by the devil. Some of the servants of God were destroyed by adultery while others were messed up because of money issues. Some were destroyed because of pride and arrogance. Putting them back together would be next to impossible if not for the grace of God. I believe you have watched some of the great preachers and tele-evangelists at one time and how they have made a wrong decision and bad judgment as they yield to Satan's temptation. Have you ever think of how much lives our enemy have destroyed and how many kids who has a great future and were destroyed, because they listened to his deceptive and convincing voice.

Satan wants to be like God and he is so desperate of man's worship. Nebuchanezzar in the Book of Daniel is a picture of what Satan is doing all over the world. Notice what Daniel said about Nebuchadnezzar in (Daniel 3: 4-7) "Then an herald cried aloud, To you it is commanded, O people, nations, and languages, 5- That at what time ye hear the sound of the cornet, flute, harp, sackbut, psaltery, dulcimer, and all kinds of music, ye fall down and worship the golden image that Nebuchadnezzar the king hath set up: 6- And whoso falleth not down and worshippeth shall the same hour be cast into the midst of a burning fiery furnace. 7- Therefore at that time, when all the people heard the sound of the cornet, flute, harp, sackbut, psaltery, and all kinds of music, all the people, the nations, and the languages, fell down and worshipped the golden image that Nebuchadnezzar the king had set up."

WEDNESDAY- MI DAILY DEVOTION
(I Peter 5:5-9)

TEMPTATION!!! TEMPTATION!!! TEMPTATION!!! UHHH!!!!

5- "Likewise, ye younger, submit yourselves unto the elder. Yea, all of you be subject one to another, and be clothed with humility: for God resisteth the proud, and giveth grace to the humble. 6- Humble yourselves therefore under the mighty hand of God, that he may exalt you in due time: 7- Casting all your care upon him; for he careth for you. 8- Be sober, be vigilant; because your adversary the devil, as a roaring lion, walketh about, seeking whom he may devour: 9- Whom resist stedfast in the faith, knowing that the same afflictions are accomplished in your brethren that are in the world."

When Satan tempted Jesus in the wilderness, he was very tricky to God. Although he knew that God will not grab and fall to his offers and generosity, he still attempted to tempt Jesus with his empty promises. This is opposite from what Christians are doing in terms of how we treat and live the Christian lives. The devil was determined to destroy Christianity even though he knew that he will never win. In Matthew 4, the devil did everything he could to make Christ his prey. But we know that he will never win and will never make Christ bow down and worship him. Satan is a loser and anyone who follows him is doomed already and is following the footsteps of a loser. The Lord mentioned it in the book of (Genesis 3:15) "And I will put enmity between thee and the woman, and between thy seed and her seed; it shall bruise thy head, and thou shalt bruise his heel." Many of us have heard of the story of Abram who was later called Abraham by God. Just after going through extremity and famine, Abraham subjected himself to temptations when he went down to Egypt and lied to Pharaoh. Satan can do and use everything including our problems to destroy us and make God looks so bad.

Satan tried to destroy Joseph, David, Solomon and God's prophets, God's servants and preachers in so many ways and tricks. He has not changed and he is still in the temptation business and working hard day and night with his destructive plans for God's children. (John 10:10) "The thief cometh not, but for to steal, and to kill, and to destroy: I am come that they might have life, and that they might have it more abundantly."

In (Genesis 12:9- 13, 17- 18) 9- "And Abram journeyed, going on still toward the south. 10- And there was a famine in the land: and Abram went down into Egypt to sojourn there; for the famine was grievous in the land. 11- And it came to pass, when he was come near to enter into Egypt, that he said unto Sarai his wife, Behold now, I know that thou art a fair woman to look upon: 12- Therefore it shall come to pass, when the Egyptians shall see thee, that they shall say, This is his wife: and they will kill me, but they will save thee alive. 13- Say, I pray thee, thou art my sister: that it may be well with me for thy sake; and my soul shall live because of thee. 17- And the LORD plagued Pharaoh and his house with great plagues because of Sarai Abram's wife. 18- And Pharaoh called Abram, and said, What is this that thou hast done unto me? why didst thou not tell me that she was thy wife?"

THURSDAY- MI DAILY DEVOTION
(Isaiah 14:12)

TEMPTATION! PRIDE! TEMPTATION! PRIDE!!!
EWWW!!!

14- "How art thou fallen from heaven, O Lucifer, son of the
morning! how art thou cut down to the ground, which didst
weaken the nations!"

Of course we know that Satan is a defeated foe even before
the world came into motion. God cast him off from heaven
to be humbled and humiliated after God found pride in
his heart. (Isaiah 14:12-19)12- "How art thou fallen from
heaven, O Lucifer, son of the morning! how art thou cut
down to the ground, which didst weaken the nations! 13- For
thou hast said in thine heart, I will ascend into heaven, I will
exalt my throne above the stars of God: I will sit also upon
the mount of the congregation, in the sides of the north: 14-
I will ascend above the heights of the clouds; I will be like
the most High. 15- Yet thou shalt be brought down to hell,
to the sides of the pit. 16- They that see thee shall narrowly
look upon thee, and consider thee, saying, Is this the man
that made the earth to tremble, that did shake kingdoms; 17-
That made the world as a wilderness, and destroyed the cities
thereof; that opened not the house of his prisoners? 18- All
the kings of the nations, even all of them, lie in glory, every
one in his own house. 19- But thou art cast out of thy grave
like an abominable branch, and as the raiment of those that
are slain, thrust through with a sword, that go down to the
stones of the pit; as a carcase trodden under feet."

You may have met different kinds of people in different
walks of life. Some Christians and preachers were humbled

by God because of pride. *SIN and PRIDE*- letter *"I"* is in the middle which for me signifies that self, selfishness and Satan is the center of such life. "I'm number 1" "I'm the greatest…" "I did it my way…" My money, my number, me first… It's always *ME, MY, MINE*. I've heard preachers preached and all they were preaching about was: *"I, ME, MY, MINE…"* They seldom talked about Jesus and His Word.

Now, let's change it to God first, my family second, my church and ministry third and others… The color of our skin will not matter as long as you serve others for the Lord's sake and for His glory. Notice what Jesus said about those selfish, self- sufficient, self- magnified Pharisees of His time and of this present time. It's so sad that people got out of focus in the ministry because of this 2 words- "temptation and pride". Sin and pride sits in because we yield on Satan's devices. Temptation is natural and it's a part of life, but pride is not. *Temptation* will always be there waiting for you, pursuing you if that's the right word, and it's haunting you. God's promised is in (I Corinthians 10:13). "There hath no temptation taken you but such as is common to man: but God is faithful, who will not suffer you to be tempted above that ye are able; but will with the temptation also make a way to escape, that ye may be able to bear it." (Matthew 7:15-20) 15- "Beware of false prophets, which come to you in sheep's clothing, but inwardly they are ravening wolves. 16- Ye shall know them by their fruits. Do men gather grapes of thorns, or figs of thistles? 17- Even so every good tree bringeth forth good fruit; but a corrupt tree bringeth forth evil fruit. 18- A good tree cannot bring forth evil fruit, neither can a corrupt tree bring forth good fruit. 19- Every tree that bringeth not forth good fruit is hewn down, and cast into the fire. 20- Wherefore by their fruits ye shall know them."

FRIDAY- MI DAILY DEVOTION
(Joshua 24:15)

"AS FOR ME AND MY HOUSE, WE WILL SERVE THE LORD"

15- "And if it seem evil unto you to serve the LORD, choose you this day whom ye will serve; whether the gods which your fathers served that were on the other side of the flood, or the gods of the Amorites, in whose land ye dwell: but as for me and my house, we will serve the LORD."

One of the Beatles' song says; "I don't know why you say goodbye, I say, hello…" This lyric of the song is expressed in many homes today. When my children were young, my wife and I always enjoyed spending time with them and being together as a family. But now that they are much older, they have become more independent. Three of them are in college and they spend more time with friends and making their own decisions. Spending time together as a family is already occasional. My message to the mothers and fathers is to spend and enjoy quality time with your children while they are still young and have them under your roof. It is especially important that you and your family are serving the Lord together. Serving God is not an option for Christians; it is a requirement with God expecting us to do our best. We can have blessings from the Lord as we serve Him faithfully. "We should walk after the LORD our God and fear him, and keep his commandments, and obey his voice, and we shall serve him, and cleave unto him." (I Samuel 12:20) "…yet turn not aside from following the LORD, but serve the LORD with all your heart;" (Joshua 24:14) "Now therefore fear the LORD, and serve him in sincerity and in truth: and put away the gods which your fathers served on the other side of the flood, and in Egypt; and serve ye the LORD."

God wants us to set aside one day a week for Him by resting from our routine and work. Set God's day apart and celebrate His blessings in the church. We have both great and small blessings in our life. Children, honor your mother and give her your best gift by coming with her to the church that preaches the gospel of the Lord Jesus Christ. My mother, before she went to be with the Lord was really faithful in the service of God. She would always get up at around 5:00 am on Sunday morning to get ready for the 6:00 am worship service and sometimes she would stay for the second service. I would suggest that families will exercise this 5 simple things each week ends: 1- Go to the same church together. 2- Prepare a good lunch or dinner for the whole family. 3- Prepare a good Christian movie. 4- Prepare something as you plan for the future. 5- Set up a good topic for conversation on the table or while relaxing. How would you and your wife like to be introduced in public like this as recorded in (Luke 1: 5-10) 5" There was in the days of Herod, the king of Judaea, a certain priest named Zacharias, of the course of Abia: and his wife was of the daughters of Aaron, and her name was Elisabeth. 6- And they were both righteous before God, walking in all the commandments and ordinances of the Lord blameless. 7- (And they had no child, because that Elisabeth was barren, and they both were now well stricken in years.) 8- And it came to pass, that while he executed the priest's office before God in the order of his course, 9- According to the custom of the priest's office, his lot was to burn incense when he went into the temple of the Lord. 10- And the whole multitude of the people were praying without at the time of incense."

SATURDAY- MI DAILY DEVOTION
(Proverbs 31:1-31)

MOTHER! MOTHER! WHO IS SICK; CALL ON JESUS VERY QUICK!

1- "The words of king Lemuel, the prophecy that his mother taught him. 31- Give her of the fruit of her hands; and let her own works praise her in the gates."

Please read the whole chapter of Proverbs 31. I preached this message on Mother's Day.

Mother, mother who is sick...? Call on Jesus very quick!!! That sounds familiar to many Filipinos. It's really familiar to many Christians. Our nation and the whole world are really sick morally, spiritually and emotionally. We have so many parents as well as children that have no moral value and very depress. There is no *LOVE* at home and that is one of the reasons why we have this sin problem and moral problems.

"The loneliest place in the world is the human heart when love is absent." (E.C. Mc Kenzie)

Here are some of the mothers in the Bible who touches the lives of their children and the people around them.

1- HANNAH, the Mother of Samuel. Hannah's prayer life- (I Samuel 1:1-31)

2- The Widow Mother who helped Elijah and became God's miracle. (I Kings 17:9-16).

3- The Widow Mother who suffered the loss of her husband? (II Kings 4:1-7).

4- Eunice the Mother of Timothy (II Timothy 1:1-6)

5- Elisabeth, the Mother of John (Luke 1:36- 80)

6- Remember Mary, the Mother of Jesus in the flesh? Mary's commitment and the sacrificed she made even before the birth of our Lord and Savior Jesus Christ, until the Lord's death on the Cross of Calvary.

7- Remember Moses' Mother?

They have learned to motivate, encourage and pray for their children. It's easier to get encouragement and motivation from someone than to encourage a son or a daughter. Timing is another issue as you encourage your children. We have known and read of great mothers who made history and because of them, their children made history and have impacted millions of lives. Do you remember your mother and did you give honor to your mother this Mother's Day? Give her a hug and a kiss and make her feel your love and care. (Isaiah 41: 7) "So the carpenter encouraged the goldsmith, and he that smootheth with the hammer him that smote the anvil, saying, It is ready for the soldering: and he fastened it with nails, that it should not be moved."

SUNDAY- MI DAILY DEVOTION
(II Kings 4:1-7)

MOTHER!!! MOTHER!!!

1- "Now there cried a certain woman of the wives of the sons of the prophets unto Elisha, saying, Thy servant my husband is dead; and thou knowest that thy servant did fear the LORD: and the creditor is come to take unto him my two sons to be bondmen. 2- And Elisha said unto her, What shall I do for thee? tell me, what hast thou in the house? And she said, Thine handmaid hath not any thing in the house, save a pot of oil. 3- Then he said, Go, borrow thee vessels abroad of all thy neighbours, even empty vessels; borrow not a few. 4- And when thou art come in, thou shalt shut the door upon thee and upon thy sons, and shalt pour out into all those vessels, and thou shalt set aside that which is full. 5- So she went from him, and shut the door upon her and upon her sons, who brought the vessels to her; and she poured out. 6- And it came to pass, when the vessels were full, that she said unto her son, Bring me yet a vessel. And he said unto her, There is not a vessel more. And the oil stayed. 7- Then she came and told the man of God. And he said, Go, sell the oil, and pay thy debt, and live thou and thy children of the rest."

MOTHER!!!! MOTHER!!!! That's what the little girl was yelling when she was in trouble. I remember watching a TV show about law enforcement. There was this big guy that got busted and he was really in big trouble. Imagine this huge guy was crying like a baby and was yelling: "Mama, please help... my God help me!!!"

In my church at the Philippine International Christian Church (PICC), I preached about this woman's situations as a mother in relation to Mother's Day celebration. Anyways, this woman lived in poverty. She was a Christian and a faithful servant of the Lord. She was not ready for the awful tragedy that comes her way by the death of her husband, a servant of God. She was the wife of the student of the prophet Elisha. It doesn't really matter who we are and how faithful we are in our service to God. We are not exempted from the problems that may come our way.

Augustine said: "Let God cover thy wounds." And that is very true, let God covers your pain and sorrow with God's love and with the comfort of the Holy Spirit. But you really have to put your trust in the Lord. But the problem with many Christians is that, we are creating our own wounds and problems. On the other hand, if you are going through trials or problems which could be your wound, you don't have to yell: "Mama, please help me!!! You say ABBA Father and tell Him your problems. It's time to exercise your faith. Let's meditate on the words of the wisest man who ever lived on earth, King Solomon: (Proverbs 3:5-6) "Trust in the LORD with all thine heart; and lean not unto thine own understanding. 6- In all thy ways acknowledge him, and he shall direct thy paths." Start it now and exercise your faith.

MONDAY- MI DAILY DEVOTION
(Hebrews 5:1; 3-4)

CHRIST THE HIGH PRIEST- *Taken from among men.*

1-"For every high priest taken from among men is ordained for men in things pertaining to God, that he may offer both gifts and sacrifices for sins:" and 3"And by reason hereof he ought, as for the people, so also for himself, to offer for sins. 4- And no man taketh this honour unto himself, but he that is called of God, as was Aaron." Mark Twain once said: "The miracle, or the power, that elevates the few is to be found in their industry, application, and perseverance under the promptings of a brave, determined spirit."

"Praise invariably implies a reference to a higher standard." Aristotle

CHRIST THE HOLY SON OF GOD. "appointed by God" (Hebrews 3:1-2) "Wherefore, holy brethren, partakers of the heavenly calling, consider the Apostle and High Priest of our profession, Christ Jesus; 2"Who was faithful to him that appointed him, as also Moses was faithful in all his house."

No one can accomplish the task but Christ Himself.

God the Father foreordained Christ even before the foundation of the world. No one can stand before God but the Lord Jesus Christ. And no one is able to do the task, but the Lord Jesus Christ. Christ is the only Messiah appointed and ordained by the Father to do the task. Christ is the Son of God. He is the Second Person of the Holy Trinity.

(Hebrews 5:4-5) 4- "And no man taketh this honour unto himself, but he that is called of God, as was Aaron. 5- So also Christ glorified not himself to be made an high priest; but he that said unto him, Thou art my Son, to day have I begotten thee,"

God Himself called Christ to the task. That's the reason why we don't have to work hard to go to heaven. That's the reason why Christ doesn't need our religion and religious rituals, because He is our religion. That's the reason why God will not weight the good versus the bad in us. God will not check our spirituality to see if we're spiritual enough for heaven. Christ is the Supreme good and the only good. He is Holy and He is God Himself. "No one is good but God" the Lord Jesus Christ said, during His encounter with the rich young ruler. Christ reconciled us to God by His death on the Cross. It's a blessing to know that the Lord Jesus Christ is our High Priest, who knew no sin and it means that we have salvation that is sure, secured, and a service to God that is sanctified. (Hebrews 2:17) 17- "Wherefore in all things it behooved him to be made like unto his brethren, that he might be a merciful and faithful high priest in things pertaining to God, to make reconciliation for the sins of the people." In the Book of (Romans 5:10) 10-"For if, when we were enemies, we were reconciled to God by the death of his Son, much more, being reconciled, we shall be saved by his life." I praise the Lord that I don't need a priest to help me go to heaven but only through the Lord Jesus Christ. We have the assurance on what He has done on the Cross. I remember what my friend said to me, "No more, no less" (II Corinthians 5:18-20) 18- "And all things are of God, who hath reconciled us to himself by Jesus Christ, and hath given to us the ministry of reconciliation; 19- "To wit, that God was in Christ, reconciling the world unto himself, not imputing their trespasses unto them; and hath committed unto us the word of reconciliation. 20- Now then we are ambassadors for Christ, as though God did beseech you by us: we pray you in Christ's stead, be ye reconciled to God."

MI DAILY DEVOTION COMMENTS

We have readers almost all over the world and we would like to share with you some of the comments we received from Facebook on the MI DAILY DEVOTION web page. We have readers from the Philippines, Israel, Japan, Singapore, Australia, Austria, United Kingdom, Denmark, Indonesia, Dubai, Saudi Arabia and the United States of America and many other countries. People who made some comments like how they were touched by the Word of God through MI DAILY DEVOTION. We did not edit their comments so pardon us for some discrepancies and words written in abbreviation. Many of those who made a comment were either in a hurry typing, it's in "text form", they are using a mobile phone or written in their own language.

Jovy Romero- thanks to you ptr,Ely whle im reading this word of God I war crying because its long time na hndi na ako nkakarining Ng salita dios my soul is very thirsty in the words of God,i knw kya ako ngkakasakit because my soul cant eat the words of GOD, -

yes ptr i do it, and thanks a lot na nasight kta even on FB i read a words of GOD by your sending me,God bless too –

thanks napakagandang mensahi realy i forget about jesus coming only my kids can remind me always they scared of they family if what will happened if our lord jesus come's today they scared also to my situation because im too much far from them, i hope everythng to me is not too late to prepared myself and my family for Jesus coming. Salamat dahl nkakabsa na ulet ako ng mga verses from the holy bible, I love u Jesus.

Danny Agpoon

Good devotional thoughts. Thanks-

Cristina Villagracia -Physical chasticement?I remember... ha ha ha.Indeed it means "Hey"Ur forgetting your creator..... Thanks Pastor Ely.Great reminder for people who have amnesia!!!!!like me at times.Honest.God Bless You Bro.-

Very true!!!!!Modern technology could either create or break a family.thanks for this reminder Pastor Ely..Your message always timely and relevant to us.Mizpaah

Thanks Pastor Ely.....Indeed chastisement is a loving correction from the Lord.PTL...been thru a lot of that!!!!!!!!!!!ha ha ha BTW Pastor my address is Cristina THanks so much

Nerissa Quinoviva Custodio - Thanks Ptr Ely for this inspiring message!God bless-

Hi Ptr Ely, your MI DAILY DEVOTION has been a channel of blessings for me when it comes to my spiritual life.How can I purchase such book?Can you deliver that to me here in Singapore?Just let me know..Thanks po!God bless

Jiccyn Nucum- Pastor Ely... just stopping by to say THANK YOU for those tagged devotions. Pls keep on doing it.-

Anna Sewel- I just finished reading a bedtime story to Erica-my little girl. ..and its the story of Samson.She told me ..Mommy,Delilah shouldnt told the secret..

She was talking about Samson's hair.Thanks Pastor for the daily tag.

Genaline Abrera Viloria amen, Pastor. A good insight and a reminder on our priorities.

idleness is satan's playground

well it is always the work of the devil to provide a seemingly good alternative to a solution God gave to our lost soul.

Dear, Pastor Ely

I borrowed some of your notes. I was so bless that i opted to share them. Thanks so much. I do appreciate sending me your notes. God bless and my prayers that many more people will be bless by your ministry.

I'll be reposting it. Thanks again. It's a blessing to me and other Christians to.

Eric Gondwe- Jesus Work Ministry- Pastor Sagansay, what a masterpiece, now in a single book!! Thank you for all the empowering messages you've shared. I trust you've been blessed as much as we have. "He who refreshes others will himself be refreshed," Proverbs 11:25. Eric Gondwe Jesus Work-Ministry

Pastor Sagansay, what a masterpiece, now in a single book!! Thank you for all the empowering messages you've shared. I trust you've been blessed as much as we have. "He who refreshes others will himself be refreshed," Proverbs 11:25.

Lookingforward to to reading your book. May God continue to use you in a mighty way. forward to to reading your book. May God continue to use you in a mighty way.

Oh great word Pastor. "...Others are so conscious of their physical position when they pray or as they pray. God is more interested in our inside attitude than with our outside expression in prayer." Amen.

forward to to reading your book. May God continue to use you in a mighty **Vivian Vicencio**- ptr, its really a blessing, coz evrytime i feel like asking something to God about trying to quit the ministry He's given me. and evertime i open your devotion, God speaks to me through the daily devotions. and praise God, i'm still in the ministry and continously serving Him. i also shares this with my choir members during our devotions. thank you very much and God bless you always. continue this for the glory of God!

Lanie Castro- That was an enlightening and enbouraging pastor. Thanks a lot.

Cora Evangelista- Thank you very much for the greetings, Thank you for being a part of my life at IBTC, Thank you for inspiring to all the daily devotion. Whatever the Lord is doing in my life now you are a pert of it. God Bless you and your family.

THANKS TO:

Dr. Celso Namuco
Lord Jesus' Stewards Fellowship Inc.
Batangas City, Philippines

Faith, Prayer and Tract League
2627 Elmridge Drive Nw, Grand Rapids, MI

Rev. Mario Merginio
Windsor, Canada

Felicidad T. E. Sagalongos. (Diksyunaryong Ingles-
Filipino, Filipino- Ingles).

Holy Bible - KJV

Merriam-Webster Dictionary, Internet

Philippine International Christian Church
4049 Longmeadow Drive
Trenton, Michigan
48183

The Bible Collection, Matthew Henry

www.nimh.nih.gov.

ENDORSEMENT:

Rev. Ely Sagansay's daily devotionals would surely touch your heart as they have to mine. They are a result of his empirical knowledge of the Scriptures. Pastor Sagansay's nearly three decades of full-time ministry as pastor/teacher is so evident in his insightful treatment of God's Word. I believe that reading this heartfelt, "God-sent" book would surely inspire, and draw one closer to God. Thank you very much, Pastor Ely. TO GOD BE THE GLORY, GREAT THINGS HE HAS DONE!

Mario Merginio
English Ministry Pastor of
Windsor Chinese Baptist Church
Windsor, Canada

MI DAILY DEVOTION of Pastor Ely Roque Sagansay is a book worth reading. Whether you are a new believer or a seasoned saint, you will gain spiritual insights from the author's nearly three decades of Christian experienced in serving the Lord. You will be encouraged and be inspired as you meditate on the truth on each page. And I hope you will be ushered to the next level of your relationship with our Lord.

Dr. Celso Namuco
Lord Jesus' Stewards Fellowship Inc.
Batangas, Philippines

ABOUT THE AUTHOR

Reverend Ely Roque Sagansay is a graduate of International Baptist Theological College of Mandaluyong, Metro Manila, Philippines. He Pastored 3 churches for almost 3 decades since he came to know the Lord Jesus Christ. Pastor Ely is a teacher, a Radio host and was the professor and administrator of International Baptist Theological College extension school in Subic Zambales. He has served as Director of music at the Greater Detroit Baptist Association and at the Philippine International Baptist Church of Taylor both in Michigan area. He is currently the Pastor of Philippine International Christian Church of Trenton, Michigan; the church he started as a church planter of the Southern Baptist Convention.

Pastor Ely was born in Bacolod City, Philippines in a Christian home and 4 of his siblings are in the Pastorate, but 1 of them went to be with the Lord.

He is married to Bermilin Dumala Sagansay and they were blessed by the Lord with 4 children; Eliezer, Ely JR, Eliel Lyn and Elmer John (EJ). His children is now serving with him in the music ministry of his church. He is a man who dearly love Missions and Missionaries. A man of God and a man for God and for His glory.